COMPASSION *and* REDEMPTION

COMPASSION *and* REDEMPTION

Celebrating *the* Women *in* Messiah's Royal Line

Miriam Nadler

Compassion and Redemption
Celebrating the Women in Messiah's Royal Line
By Miriam Nadler

©2018 by Miriam Nadler
All rights Reserved.
ISBN: 978-1728870656

Contents

Foreword	1
From the Author	3
Introduction	5

Tamar
1.	An Unlikely Dysfunctional Family	16
2.	From Mourning to Dancing	25
3.	Do You Need a Breakthrough?	35

Rahab
4.	Before the Walls Came Tumbling Down	46
5.	From Harlot to Heroine	57
6.	Do You Need a Hero?	66

Ruth
7.	A Famine in the House of Bread!	74
8.	Where Did She Get Such Courage?	80
9.	The Servant of the Lord Came for You	96

Bathsheba
10.	No Stranger to the Palace	104
11.	From Grief to Grace	108
12.	A Greater Than Solomon is Here	124

Miriam
13.	A Time of Miracles	132
14.	Her Humble Heart Revealed	137
15.	My King of Kings	151

Bibliography	161

Foreword

Compassion and Redemption: Celebrating the Women in Messiah's Royal Line is the result of studies I was privileged to lead at Hope of Israel Congregation. Realizing how the lives of the women from Matthew's genealogy offered hope and insight into the grace of God, I wanted to make this material available in book form. It's been almost a five-year journey, and there are many people to thank.

My husband Sam continually inspired me to stay focused on completing this project. Wendy Bowen's feedback and encouragement with the first draft was invaluable. Shari, Laurel and Gloria edited and shared their ideas after reading the first of many drafts.

What really helped to push me over the finish line was the group of committed ladies who met weekly for six months to study the material together. This diverse collection of ladies—of all ages and walks of life—responded to the material in unique ways, offering helpful feedback. Thanks to all of them for their involvement in making this book a reality. Special thanks goes out to Laurie, Stacy, Rachel, Donna, Barbara, Kaf, Rhonda, Cynthia, Katherine, Sylvia, Susie, Maribel, Gail, Andrea, Jenny, Judith, Mary Lou, Vickie, Kelsey and Debi. And much gratitude to Madelyn, Leslie and Joy for their help with the final draft!

Finally, all praise and honor belongs to Yeshua my Messiah! I am eternally thankful for His compassion, redemption and faithfulness.

From the Author

During my college years as a very young believer, I was discipled by Arnold Fruchtenbaum, a Jewish believer in Jesus and founder of Ariel Ministries. In me Arnold saw ministry potential, even though I was very immature and untaught in the Scriptures. He encouraged me in all aspects of the faith, including believing God to provide for my school bill as I worked my way through college, and imparting an understanding and love for the Jewish people. To help me grow in that understanding, he recommended that I write my papers for English and History on various aspects of Jewish life, especially the Holocaust. I became involved in Arnold's prayer group for Israel, and the Lord put a burden on my heart to reach out to Jewish people.

I spent four summers ministering in Brooklyn, New York with Hilda Koser, who was one of the great Jewish missionaries for Messiah. As I worked alongside her during the summer Bible school outreaches in Coney Island, NY, Miss Koser taught me how to minister to children.

The Lord provided another mentor in Ruth Wardell, a Gentile believer in Messiah whose impact for the Lord among Jewish young people was profound. As a counselor at Camp Sar Shalom for Jewish teens, I watched Ruth interact with them. With her example and encouragement and by God's grace, I was able to have a positive impact on the lives of a number of young women as a counselor and Bible teacher.

After graduating from Cedarville University with a degree in teaching, I knew that the Lord was calling me into Jewish ministry. For a short time, I taught in public school to pay off my college loans; then, with great joy and anticipation I moved to New York City to work with Chosen People Ministries (the American Board of Missions to the Jews) where I studied under Moishe Rosen who later founded Jews for Jesus.

COMPASSION *and* REDEMPTION

I immersed myself in Jewish culture, learned the Hebrew language and soaked up Israeli music. I began a small women's Bible study that met Friday evenings on the Upper West Side. I would often cook a meal for about a dozen ladies who gathered for study and discipleship. At only 21 years old, it was my first experience teaching a women's Bible study to these amazing women who represented a variety of ages and professions.

After three years of ministry in New York City, I had the privilege of moving to Israel, where I studied at Hebrew University in Jerusalem for a year. I attended an ulpan, an immersive Hebrew language program. That year in Israel turned out to be not merely a time to study but a time to minister. Through one-on-one friendships and a coffee house outreach in Jerusalem that I helped to start, the Lord provided many opportunities to share my faith. After that life-changing year in Israel, I returned to New York City.

Shortly after, the Lord led me to move to California to help start Jews for Jesus and lead the newly-formed musical outreach called The Liberated Wailing Wall. There I met a new believer named Sam Nadler. The Lord brought us together in love and in ministry.

For the first few years of our married lives, we were on the road, criss-crossing the USA doing concerts for both evangelistic outreach and deputation. When our touring days ended, Sam and I moved to New York City to open the New York branch of Jews for Jesus. I jumped right in, discipling women both individually and in small groups.

Sam and I became increasingly convinced that discipling needed to be in the context of a congregational community. In 1979 Sam accepted the position of Northeast Regional Director of Chosen People Ministries where together with the New York area staff we started Messianic Congregations in Westchester, Long Island, Connecticut, and New Jersey. We saw a number of people not only make decisions for the Lord but also be discipled and grow in their faith.

In 1989, we moved our two sons, Josh and Matt, to Charlotte, NC, where Sam led the ministry of CPM in their new headquarters for the next seven years. These were fruitful years as we saw the Lord open the doors to reach Russian Jews in the former Soviet Union. During these years, we helped plant congregations in the cities of Kiev, Ukraine and Berlin, Germany, to name a few. As Sam mentored and coached these new congregational leaders, I had the privilege of mentoring several of the leader's wives.

Then, in 1997, Sam and I founded Word of Messiah Ministries to concentrate on planting and strengthening Messianic congregations by developing practical discipleship materials and implementing proven programs. I still consider the opportunity to disciple women and develop teaching materials a special calling of God and am thankful for ongoing opportunities to see the lives of women transformed by the Word of God.

For Messiah's Glory,
Miriam Nadler

Introduction

Let's begin our study with a few questions:

1. Have you ever felt like an outcast, spurned by your community?
2. Did an influential person ever make a promise to you and then break it, never intending to keep his word?
3. Have you gone through the crushing grief of losing a spouse or a child?
4. Have you ever been forced to take a disappointing job to support your extended family?
5. Do you ever feel vulnerable, unappreciated or disdained by family or friends?

If you responded in the affirmative to any of these questions, this book is for you!

I love studying and teaching the Scriptures to women of all ages. Like many of us, I tend to steer away from the long genealogies, glossing over them with a quick read, avoiding the names that look too difficult to pronounce. Recently however, reading through Matthew Chapter One, I decided to investigate the women mentioned in the genealogy of Yeshua (the Hebrew way to say Jesus) to try and find a common thread or theme among them. Although I had taught individual studies on a few of these women, I had never approached this portion as a whole to explore their commonality and discover how it relates to us. I wondered if such a study would be encouraging to women providing additional insight for practical living. However, my own encouragement grew to astonishment and transformed into thanksgiving to God for His amazing grace expressed in the lives of these women and their offspring, and finally to me. It became clear that Tamar, Rahab, Ruth, Bathsheba, and Miriam were strong and brave individuals who became instrumental in bringing salvation to the world.

If we were to examine these women from a human perspective, a first glance might reveal Tamar the Canaanite, Rahab the harlot, Ruth the Moabite, Bathsheba the wife of Uriah the Hittite, and Miriam the unwed mother to be "throw away people." None of them would be under consideration for a Nobel Peace Prize or Time magazine's "Person of the Year." Tamar had been betrayed and twice widowed. Rahab was compelled to make a living by sleeping with strangers. Ruth found herself widowed and penniless. Bathsheba was coerced into having sex with King David. And Miriam of the Gospels was a poor pregnant teenager with no influence and no place to stay to have her baby. As we study each of their stories, we will see how God entered their hopeless situations to make each one His vessel of grace and a unique instrument for redemption. Transforming their circumstance, God gave each one a purpose beyond what they could have ever imagined.

It is my prayer that the women of Matthew, Chapter One, will find a way into your soul and offer you divine inspiration and that this study will help you observe the redemptive flow of history, as orchestrated by our Creator. I pray that through the eyes of God's grace, you will recognize yourself as a woman of valor in Yeshua, who continues to live out His redemptive story for the world all around you and that this will be our focus as we seek to honor Yeshua the Messiah in all we do.

What Is a Genealogy?

The word genealogy is synonymous with a "family tree," lineage, pedigree or ancestry. Webster's dictionary offers two simple definitions:

1. The study of family history
2. The history of a specific family showing how the different members of the family are related to each other

In fact, if you did a Google search on the word genealogy, you would find a plethora of websites where people who have an interest in knowing their heritage can search and discover information about their family

INTRODUCTION

ancestry. Maybe you have visited one of these sites to explore your own history. It's possible that you expected to find a heroic or brave figure in your line of forebears. Perhaps you were secretly hoping to discover that you were a descendant of nobility and that a vast estate in Europe awaits your claim! If I were to explore my lineage it would be with the hope of finding courageous and exemplary people instead of unsavory characters.

Today exploring one's family history is often just a curiosity or hobby. Realistically speaking, would new information regarding my ancestry actually effect my present life? If, by some miracle I were to discover wealthy or famous relatives, it would probably not make much difference in how I live my daily life. Unfortunately, however, many people still try to find validation by pursuing information about their ancestry.

FOR ANCIENT ISRAEL, ANCESTRAL RECORDS DID MATTER!

On the other hand, for those who lived in ancient Israel, knowing what tribe and people they belonged to was essential; affecting every area of life. Ancestral records generally recorded the line of descendants from father to son. These genealogies were vigilantly preserved, for the purposes of tribal land ownership. From these records birthrights were determined. There are many Scripture references that address the rights of inheritance (1 Chronicles 5:1,17 9:1, 2 Chronicles 12:15, Ezra 2:62).

When the Jewish people returned to Israel following the seventy years of captivity in Babylon that began in 586 BCE, one of the things they did—along with rebuilding the temple, the city and the walls—was to collect all the genealogical records which had been carefully kept and remained preserved until all records were destroyed when the Roman general Titus Vespasian destroyed Jerusalem in 70 AD. As a result, today there is no way to really trace one's lineage before the time of the Temple's destruction.

> "The [Hebrew] Rabbis affirm that after the [Babylonian] Captivity the Jews were most careful in keeping their pedigrees (Babyl. Gemar. Gloss. fol. xiv, 2). Since, however, the period of their destruction as a nation by the Romans, all their tables of descent seem to be lost, and now they are utterly unable to trace the pedigree of anyone who might lay claim to be their promised Messiah"[1] (3.771; emp.WJ).

---

[1] McClintock, John & James Strong. *Cyclopedia of Biblical, Theological, and Ecclesiastical Literature*. Grand Rapids: Baker. 1969.

COMPASSION *and* REDEMPTION

NEW COVENANT RECORDS

In the genealogies of Matthew and Luke, we find evidence that Messiah Yeshua was born according to prophecy of the seed of Abraham, making him heir to the throne of Israel as the greater son of David. How miraculous that the public records of the genealogies were kept secure for more than 2000 years of turbulent history until the Temple was destroyed. (1 Chronicles 1–8)

Even more remarkable is the fact that the destruction of these records happened approximately 37 years after Messiah's resurrection and ascension back to heaven. Yeshua's coming changed everything as He ushered in a new family heritage and genealogy for all who would believe. In Him, we are declared to be children of the most High God. The apostle John affirms this in 1 John 3:1, declaring, see how great a love the Father has bestowed upon us, that we should be called children of God; and such we are.

Matthew's genealogy follows the line of Joseph of the New Testament, whose father was Jacob, himself a descendant of David's son Solomon through the royal line. Luke's genealogy follows the line of Miriam of the New Testament, whose father was Heli, a descendant of David's son Nathan. The bloodline recorded by Matthew begins with Abraham and continues to David, then, through the line of Solomon, to Joseph of Nazareth. Given his ancestry, Joseph might have been a king. However, because, he was a descendant of King Jehoiachin, Joseph was barred from the throne by divine prohibition as was declared by the prophet Jeremiah. (Jeremiah 22:30) Instead of being royalty, Joseph was a village carpenter.

It was clear that a different son of David, not descended from the accursed Jehoiachin line, must be the one to sit on the throne. Though Yeshua was legally adopted by Joseph as his legitimate son, his claim as rightful heir to the throne of David came through His mother Miriam, who was also descended from the house of David. Each line—that of Joseph and that of Miriam—fulfilled the prophecy promising that the Messiah would descend from the line of David.

For our study, we will consider the question of why Matthew included five women in his genealogy of Messiah Yeshua—records usually consisting of only patriarchal lineage. Perhaps Matthew wanted to remind us that the first promise of Scripture foretold the coming of the Redeemer, born of the seed of the woman (Genesis 3:15). It would make sense, then, to include women in Messiah's genealogy.

INTRODUCTION

If Matthew wanted to include women in his records, the first verse would have been a perfect time to mention Abraham's wife, Sarah. Yet he began, The book of the genealogy of Jesus the Messiah, the son of David, the son of Abraham. (Matthew 1:1) Perhaps Matthew had another purpose in mind, because the women he included reveal Messiah Yeshua, not only as the King of Israel, but also as Savior of the world. To this end, Matthew deliberately includes two Canaanite women, one Moabite woman, an Israelite woman who married a Hittite, and one teenage Jewish girl, offering us a foretaste of what Messiah came to accomplish for the whole world—both men and women.

WOMEN ARE HEIRS AND JOINT HEIRS WITH THE KING OF KINGS! When we consider the heritage and rights in our families of origin, whether in a patriarchal society or a matriarchal society, we are always headed down a dysfunctional path except for the grace of God. Only by personal faith in Yeshua's atonement can we find our place in Messiah's eternally functional family. Here on earth we can live as His child with all the rights and privileges of His divine calling, as we let our lights shine to reflect his greater light into the members of our earthly families.

The apostle Paul reiterates this.

> The Spirit Himself bears witness with our spirit that we are children of God, and if children, heirs also, heirs of God and fellow heirs with Messiah, if indeed we suffer with Him in order that we may also be glorified with Him.   —Romans 8:16–17

Yeshua gives each of us His genealogy. From the very beginning of John's Gospel, he explains that if we receive Yeshua as the promised Messiah and Savior, we will become His children.

> But as many as received Him, to them He gave the right to become children of God, even to those who believe in His name, who were born not of blood, nor of the will of the flesh, nor of the will of man, but of God.   —John 1:12–13

See how great a love the Father has bestowed upon us, that we should be called children of God; and such we are. For this reason, the world does not know us, because it did not know Him. Beloved, now we are children of God, and it has not appeared as yet what we shall be. We know that, when He appears, we shall be like Him, because we shall see Him just as He is. —1 John 3:1–2

It was always God's plan to bring us back into His family by His love and mercy. We are by adoption, blessed with every spiritual blessing in the heavenly places in Messiah. The Apostle Paul explains our genealogy of grace in his letter to the Ephesians.

> Blessed be the God and Father of our Lord Yeshua the Messsiah, who has blessed us with every spiritual blessing in the heavenly places in Messiah, just as He chose us in Him before the foundation of the world, that we should be holy and blameless before Him. In love He predestined us to adoption as sons through Yeshua the Messiah to Himself, according to the kind intention of His will, to the praise of the glory of His grace, which He freely bestowed on us in the Beloved. —Ephesians 1:3–6

When you trust in Messiah, He forgives your past, while transforming your present and your future by giving you eternal life now and forever.

Let's discover together how Messiah takes women whom many would call "throw-away people" and transforms them. Yeshua wants you to understand His transforming power in you. Your Beloved Messiah desires for you to know who you are in Him, because you are His beloved daughter, now and for eternity.

About this Book

There are five sections which correspond with the five women in the genealogy of Matthew. Each section contains three chapters, which include the historical setting, a study of the woman and how her son foreshadowed the Messiah Yeshua.

For example:

Section One: Tamar

1. An Unlikely Dysfunctional Family (historical setting for Tamar)
2. From Mourning to Dancing (the life of Tamar)
3. Do You Need a Breakthrough in your Life? (Tamar's son and Messiah's fulfillment)

INTRODUCTION

Each chapter includes discussion questions which can be utilized in personal study or group gatherings. Instead of searching the web for more information on your earthly heritage let's search the Scriptures to discover the grace of His eternal genealogy.

SECTION ONE

תמר
TAMAR

"and to Judah was
born Peretz...
by Tamar"
Matthew 1:3

COMPASSION *and* REDEMPTION

1. An Unlikely Dysfunctional Family!

The women in Matthew's genealogy span much of Israel's history. Tamar is the first woman recorded in this lineage. We meet her while Jacob and his sons are still becoming the twelve tribes of Israel. Let's take a brief look at the beginnings of this family, which is so pivotal to God's plan of redemption. In Genesis 27, we read of the stolen blessing, which Rebekah instigated, arranging for her second son, Jacob, to receive the blessings of the firstborn from his frail and blind father Isaac. When Jacob's older brother, Esau, discovered that he had been deceived and cheated out of his birthright, he wanted to kill Jacob. Jacob fled the scene to find a wife from the family of Rebekah's brother Laban. In Genesis 29, we meet Laban and his two daughters, Rachel and Leah. These sisters, along with their handmaidens, gave Jacob twelve sons who became the twelve tribes of Israel.

Poetic Justice?

Deception is a central theme in the origins of this family of twelve sons which God would form into the twelve tribes of Israel. First younger brother Jacob steals the birthright of the firstborn by pretending to be his older brother Esau. Next, Laban deceives Jacob by substituting his older daughter Leah for Jacob's beloved Rachel, for whom Jacob had worked for seven years. Jacob awoke from his marriage bed to find his heavily veiled wife was not the woman he was promised. This is an example of the Scriptural principle "what you sow you will reap." Some might call it poetic justice as Jacob found himself on the receiving end of a deception by his father-in-law. What about Leah who felt unloved and Rachel who was greatly loved by Jacob? It might appear that Laban, instead of being a loving father to his girls, used them as pawns to enrich himself with Jacob's extra seven years of service before finally receiving his beloved Rachel as his wife?

Yet we can discover from Scripture that God, in spite of deception on the part of his children, poured out his love and grace upon both Leah and Rachel. Remember as you consider their situations, God wants to pour out His grace and love to you as well.

> Now the LORD saw that Leah was unloved, and He opened her womb, but Rachel was barren. And Leah conceived and bore a son and named him Reuben, for she said, "Because the LORD has seen my affliction; surely now my husband will love me."
>
> —Genesis 29: 31, 32

Do you believe that God understands your buried hurts and unspoken prayers? The Lord knew what Leah needed and gave her Reuben, the firstborn of the twelve sons. In turn, Leah acknowledged that the LORD had taken notice of her affliction and had provided for her. Still, Leah was not satisfied to be blessed with a son by the LORD, because her deepest desire was to be loved by her husband. Hoping that a child would stir Jacob's heart, Leah says, "surely now my husband will love me."

This longing persists even after the births of Simeon and Levi.

> Then she conceived again and bore a son and said, "Because the LORD has heard that I am unloved, He has therefore given me this son also." So, she named him Simeon. And she conceived again and bore a son and said, "Now this time my husband will become attached to me, because I have borne him three sons." Therefore, he was named Levi.
> —Genesis 29:33, 34

The *Complete Jewish Bible* puts it this way:

> Once more [Leah] conceived and had a son; and she said, "Now this time my husband will be joined to me, because I have borne him three sons." Therefore she named him Levi [joining].
> —Genesis 29:34 (CJB)

Not satisfied with God's love and care, Leah continued to look for that unrequited love from Jacob.

How Did Judah Receive His Name?

How does Judah fit into the birth order? I found it very meaningful to understand how Judah received his name. When Leah gave birth to her fourth son she declared that it was time for her to praise the LORD, so she named him Judah or Y'hudah—praiser of God," from the root, *yadah*, which means to throw, to revere, to worship God.

> And she conceived again and bore a son and said, "This time I will praise the LORD." Therefore she named him Judah, Y'hudah [praise].
> — Genesis 29:35

COMPASSION *and* REDEMPTION

It's important to note that during this time a battle continued between Leah and Rachel as they competed for Jacob's attention and affection. We know Rachel's mindset.

> Now when Rachel saw that she bore Jacob no children, she became jealous of her sister; and she said to Jacob, "Give me children, or else I die." Then Jacob's anger burned against Rachel, and he said, "Am I in the place of God, who has withheld you the fruit of the womb?" —Genesis 30:1–2

In Genesis 30: 7–8 we read that Naphtali was born to Rachel's surrogate, her handmaid Bilhah, till the Lord remembered Rachel, opened her womb and she gave birth to Joseph. One more time Rachel became pregnant but dies giving birth to their youngest son. As she was dying Rachel wanted to call her son Ben-oni—child of my sorrow, but Jacob named him Benjamin—son of my right hand.

Despite the rivalry and bad blood between the wives and their children in their struggle for Jacob's affections, Rachel remained the true bride of Jacob's heart. Her son Joseph was clearly Jacob's favorite and his youngest, Benjamin, also held a very special place in his heart.

Now we will move forward and turn our attention to Jacob and Leah's son Judah, who is a grown man. We join him in the midst of a family crisis as Jacob's sons plot to kill their younger brother Joseph.

> Israel loved Joseph more than all of his other sons, because he was the son of his old age. So, he made him a long-sleeved tunic.
> —Genesis 37:3 (TLV)

By giving Joseph this decorative and finely woven coat, Jacob set Joseph apart from his brothers and elevated his status in the family. This favoritism toward Joseph incurred the hostility of his brothers. Then an occasion to punish Joseph arises when Jacob instructs his seventeen-year-old son to check on his brothers who were away, caring for the sheep. Joseph's job was to report back to Jacob anything unsavory that was going on. Jealousy and resentment overcame Joseph's brothers, and they were determined to get rid of their annoying sibling. Instead of killing him outright, Judah makes arrangements for Joseph to be sold into slavery.

TAMAR

> And Judah said to his brothers, "What profit is it for us to kill our brother and cover up his blood? Come and let us sell him to the Ishmaelite's and not lay our hands on him; for he is our brother, our own flesh." Judah's brothers listened to him.
> —Genesis 37:26–27

After the sons sold Joseph, they dipped his special coat in blood to make it appear that their brother had been killed. When news of Joseph's death reached Jacob, he is engulfed in sorrow. The Scriptures are so descriptive that one can feel Jacob's overwhelming anguish.

> Then Jacob examined it and said, "It is my son's tunic. A wild beast has devoured him; Joseph has surely been torn to pieces!" So Jacob tore his clothes, and put sackcloth on his loins, and mourned for his son many days. Then all his sons and all his daughters arose to comfort him, but he refused to be comforted. And he said, "Surely I will go down to Sheol in mourning for my son." So his father wept for him.
> —Genesis 37:33–35

Jacob's immediate response to the death of Joseph was to tear his own clothes and cover himself in sackcloth to express his inner anguish and inconsolable grief. Joseph, the first-born of his beloved Rachel, was gone, and Jacob's plans for Joseph were destroyed. (Genesis 30: 22–24)

IS THIS THE END OF THE LINE?

As Jacob's sorrow permeated his home, it is not surprising that Judah who was the "ring leader" of this deceitful situation would want to disappear as quickly as possible. He leaves home to settle among the Canaanites.

> And it came about at that time that Judah departed from his brothers, and visited a certain Adullamite, whose name was Hirah.
> —Genesis 38:1

The purpose of our study is not to go into the evil practices that were common in the debased Canaanite society. However, because their sin was so great, the Lord eventually commands the Israelites to utterly destroy them. The Scripture describes the Lord's judgment on the various nations including the Canaanites, who practice all sorts of abominable things:

> "But you shall utterly destroy them, the Hittite and the Amorite, the Canaanite and the Perizzite, the Hivite and the Jebusite, as the LORD your God has commanded you, in order that they may not teach you to do according to all their detestable things which they have done for their gods, so that you would sin against the LORD your God."
> — Deuteronomy 20:17–18

The fact that Judah went to dwell among the Canaanites could have signaled the end of his line. Consider for a moment what would have happened if Judah had married a Canaanite woman, raised his children as Canaanites, and remained there, forsaking the God of his fathers. Because, according to Genesis 49:10, the Messiah had to come from the tribe of Judah, the assimilation of Judah's offspring into a pagan culture may have diabolically ended the Messianic line. This prophecy is recorded in the blessing that Jacob gave to his son Judah.

> "The scepter shall not depart from Jacob, nor the ruler's staff from his feet, until Shiloh comes, and to him shall be the obedience of the peoples." —Genesis 49:10

Despite Judah's initial disobedience, God's providential hand was working all things together to preserve His people and His promises.

A Glimpse Forward in History

One description of providence is "God's hand in the glove of history." Another more complete definition is found in the *Baker's Evangelical Dictionary of Biblical Theology*: Providence is the sovereign superintendence of all things, guiding them toward their divinely predetermined end in a way that is consistent with their created nature. This divine, sovereign and benevolent control of all things by God is the underlying premise of everything that is taught in the Scriptures.[1]

Remember how Judah, the ringleader, had schemed with his brothers to sell Joseph instead of killing him? Right here in the narrative of the

---

[1] *Baker's Evangelical Dictionary of Biblical Theology*. Edited by Walter A. Elwell, ©1996 by Walter A. Elwell. Published by Baker Books

beginnings of the nation of Israel we observe God's providential hand. That Joseph was sold as a slave and ended up in Egypt was not a surprise to God; on the contrary, the Lord had placed His servant there in order to eventually give him a position of great power, allowing Joseph to not only save his family from famine but to bring them down to Egypt to grow and thrive as the community of Israel. In all of it, God's providential hand was working.

Genesis 37 reveals this low point of disgrace for Judah; nonetheless, we recognize that God achieves His purpose through everyday sinners like Abraham and Sarah, Jacob and Leah—and even sinners like you and me. As we look at that early part of Israel's history, we can be encouraged by how God was working all things together to fulfill His redemptive purposes through the line of Judah. We can praise God's faithfulness for keeping Jacob and the sons of Israel central to His providential plan, in spite of themselves.

> The LORD positioned Joseph in Egypt, promoting this lowly slave to a status second only to the Pharaoh. Joseph reveals his true identity to his trembling brothers. Then Joseph said to his brothers, "Please come closer to me." And they came closer. And he said, "I am your brother Joseph, whom you sold into Egypt. And now do not be grieved or angry with yourselves, because you sold me here; for God sent me before you to preserve life. For the famine has been in the land these two years, and there are still five years in which there will be neither plowing nor harvesting. And God sent me before you to preserve for you a remnant in the earth, and to keep you alive by a great deliverance. Now, therefore, it was not you who sent me here, but God; and He has made me a father to Pharaoh and lord of all his household and ruler over all the land of Egypt."
> —Genesis 45:4–8

Notice verses seven and eight. Joseph explains to his brothers that God had sent him to Egypt and given him power to fulfill His own redemptive purposes—"to keep the remnant alive."

Judah and his brothers humbled themselves and repented. After they buried their father Jacob, the brothers were terrified that Joseph would seek retribution. They reminded Joseph of their father's plea for him to forgive them and repented again.

COMPASSION *and* REDEMPTION

> So they sent a message to Joseph, saying, "Your father charged before he died, saying, 'Thus you shall say to Joseph, "Please forgive, I beg you, the transgression of your brothers and their sin, for they did you wrong."' And now, please forgive the transgression of the servants of the God of your father." And Joseph wept when they spoke to him. Then his brothers also came and fell down before him and said, "Behold, we are your servants." —Genesis 50:16–18

How does Joseph respond to his brothers? He reminds them all of God's providential care for both himself and their entire family.

> But Joseph said to them, "Do not be afraid, for am I in God's place? "And as for you, you meant evil against me, but God meant it for good in order to bring about this present result, to preserve many people alive. —Genesis 50:19–20

The New Covenant reiterates how the God of Joseph and Judah continues to work all things together for good to those who love Him and are called according to His purpose, unfolding the details of our lives to bring about His plans and purposes.

> And we know that God causes all things to work together for good to those who love God, to those who are called according to His purpose. —Romans 8:28

It's important to remember that when God is bringing all the circumstances of our lives together for good, it means everything in our lives, including the difficulties, trials and sorrows. When we entrust every situation into His hands He causes even trying circumstances to resolve for His purposes and for our good.

THE PROMISE OF REDEMPTION

Judah's ongoing appalling behavior continues throughout the narrative of Genesis 38. But it only serves to demonstrate God's grace. Despite his weaknesses and lack of character, Judah is given more chances to get it right. Before he dies, Jacob gives Judah a blessing declaring how his son will be used to glorify and praise the Lord. In Genesis 49, we find a prophecy of Messiah's coming in this blessing—a valuable lesson in understanding how God works in the lives of His people. We mentioned Genesis 49:10 previously, but now let's look further into the context of this verse and the entire blessing Jacob bestows upon Judah:

> "Judah, your brothers shall praise you; Your hand shall be on the neck of your enemies; Your father's sons shall bow down to you. Judah is a lion's whelp (cub); From the prey, my son, you have gone up. He couches, he lies down as a lion, and as a lion, who dares rouse him up? The scepter shall not depart from Judah, Nor the ruler's staff from between his feet, Until Shiloh comes, and to him shall be the obedience of the peoples." —Genesis 49:8–10

In verse 8, Jacob prophesies that Judah will live up to his name—praiser of God. Judah became the head of the royal tribe that gave Israel their kings and the King of kings, Yeshua the Messiah.

> For it is evident that our Lord was descended from Judah.
> —Hebrews 7:14

Judah's was the tribe that remained faithful to the Davidic line even when Israel became a divided kingdom. In Verse 9, Jacob declared that his son will be like a lion, both as a young cub and as a mature lion who would protect and defend his people. This description calls to mind the heavenly scene described in Revelation—a picture of the Lion of the Tribe of Judah. In this portion of Revelation chapter 5, John is distraught that no one is worthy to break the seals and open the book. An angel comforts John.

> "Stop weeping; behold, the Lion that is from the tribe of Judah, the Root of David, has overcome so as to open the book and its seven seals." —Revelation 5:5

The prophecy of Messiah Yeshua in Genesis 49:10 says that the ruling scepter would continue to be from the line of Judah until Shiloh comes. There are many interpretations and speculations concerning whom this Shiloh might be. The Hebrew translation for Shiloh is simply "he whose it is" or "until he comes whose right it is" meaning, the right to rule. In ancient rabbinical writings, Shiloh was always considered to

COMPASSION *and* REDEMPTION

be a name for Messiah. (Isaiah 11:10) Praise the Lord, in the fullness of time, King Messiah did come. He is the only One who will command the obedience of all peoples as both the prophets and the New Covenant proclaim:

> "I have sworn by Myself, the word has gone forth from My mouth in righteousness And will not turn back, That to Me every knee will bow, every tongue will swear allegiance." —Isaiah 45:23

> "Therefore also God highly exalted Him, and bestowed on Him the name which is above every name, that at the name of Yeshua every knee should bow, of those who are in heaven, and on earth, and under the earth, and that every tongue should confess that Yeshua the Messiah is Lord, to the glory of God the Father."
> —Philippians 2:9–11

Questions, Thoughts and Reflections

1. Take time to give God praise for His providential care which has brought you to this place in your life and which continues to shape your life. Review the portions from Genesis 50:19–20 and Romans 8:28. How do you see God revealing these truths in your own life?

2. Write down the ways that the Lord has been faithful to forgive you when you mess up. Offer praise and thanks to the Lord even as King David suggests in Psalm 103.

Bless the Lord, O my soul; And all that is within me, bless His holy name. Bless the Lord, O my soul, and forget none of His benefits; Who pardons all your iniquities; Who heals all your diseases; Who redeems your life from the pit; Who crowns you with lovingkindness and compassion; Who satisfies your years with good things, So that your youth is renewed like the eagle.
—Psalm 103:1–5

TAMAR

2. From Mourning to Dancing

Now that we have reviewed some of the background of Judah and his family, let's consider how Tamar, a Canaanite, and her son have received the privilege of being recorded in the lineage of Yeshua the Messiah, the Lion of the tribe of Judah. This seems impossible, because when we meet Judah in Genesis 38, he is not a mighty leader but more like the character of the Cowardly Lion from the Wizard of Oz. As we take a closer look at Genesis 38, it's my prayer that we will understand how Tamar and her son became forever honored by grace as part of the royal genealogy of Messiah Yeshua.

> And it came about at that time, that Judah departed from his brothers, and visited a certain Adullamite, whose name was Hirah.
> —Genesis 38:1

While Joseph's father was engulfed in grief, Judah, who had instigated the sale of his brother Joseph and the deception his father Jacob, was probably engulfed in guilt. He hoped that moving away from his father and brothers to live among the Canaanites would put distance between him and his family.

Fleeing his dreadful deeds, Judah seeks a new life. He marries Shua, a Canaanite woman and has three sons: Er, Onan and Shelah. No mention is made of Judah seeking the Lord as he continues to live his life.

Judah chooses a woman named Tamar to be the wife for his firstborn son, Er. In Genesis 38:7 we read; "But Er, Judah's first-born, was evil in the sight of the LORD, so the LORD took his life." The common Hebrew word for evil (*raah*) used in this verse means to act wickedly and do harm. The Scriptures do not explain Er's evil deeds, but the language is clear; they were so horrendous that the LORD took his life.

According to the custom of the day, which later became codified in the law of Moses, (see Deuteronomy 25:5-10) when an older brother dies his younger brother must take his wife as his own in order to honor his brother's name and raise up children to keep his brother's memory alive. Er's brother, Onan was in line to marry Tamar to carry on the family name for his deceased brother. The Scripture explains what happened:

> Then Judah said to Onan, "Go in to your brother's wife, and perform your duty as a brother-in-law to her, and raise up offspring for

COMPASSION *and* REDEMPTION

> your brother." And Onan knew that the offspring would not be his; so, it came about that when he went in to his brother's wife, he wasted his seed on the ground, in order not to give offspring to his brother. But what he did was displeasing in the sight of the LORD; so He took his life also. —Genesis 38:8–10

What Onan did was so evil in God's eyes He took his life on the spot. Onan demonstrated a loveless attitude toward his brother and ignored his father's request to raise up his dead brother's seed, disregarding the custom of the day. This heartless and selfish view was reprehensible to the Lord. Spilling his seed on the ground brought immediate judgment and a death sentence from the LORD.

Two Down and One to Go

Judah had one remaining son, Shelah, who was too young to fulfill the brotherly obligation to carry on the family name. But at this same time, Judah began to wonder if Tamar was the reason his two sons were dead.

> Then Judah said to his daughter-in-law Tamar, "Remain a widow in your father's house until my son Shelah grows up," for he thought, "I am afraid that he too may die like his brothers." So Tamar went and lived in her father's house. —Genesis 38:11

Judah's fear over Tamar led him to make her a promise that he never intended to keep. He tells her to live in her father's house, and not in his home. Could it be that Judah does not want Tamar around his son Shelah? Judah also tells Tamar to keep wearing the clothing of a widow, promising that when Shelah is of marrying age then she will be able to remove her widow's garb, marry Shelah and have her own family.

At first, Tamar believes Judah and she returns to her father's house. However, in Genesis 38:12 we are told that after a considerable amount of time had past and Tamar understood that even though Shelah was now old enough to marry her, Judah had no intention of fulfilling his promise.

Taking Matters into Her Own Hands

Remember how Judah had encouraged his brothers to sell Joseph into slavery, then covered Joseph's tunic in blood resulting in Jacob's inconsolable grief? Now Judah had lost two sons and a wife of his own and could truly sympathize with his father's sorrow. At any point, Judah could have opened his heart to God's forgiveness, comfort and guidance. But instead of seeking the Lord, Judah decides that Tamar is the problem and that his youngest son Shelah must be kept away from her.

Judah wrongly blames Tamar when it is he who married a Canaanite woman and who encouraged his son to do the same. Why didn't Judah repent of his sins and turn back to the God of his fathers?

Tamar's Predicament: We Empathize but cannot Justify

What about Tamar, married and widowed by two men whom the Scriptures describe as doing evil in the sight of God? She was lied to by Judah, leaving her no recourse. Stuck in her father's house, forced to wear her widow's clothes with no end in sight. How did Tamar feel? Unloved, rejected, humiliated, betrayed, angry, grief stricken, and trapped in a dead-end situation?

The Scripture is silent concerning what Tamar's life was like in her father's household, but we do have historical data about life in a Canaanite home, and it is not a pretty picture. Certainly Tamar longed to remove her clothes of mourning. And her subsequent actions confirm a deep longing to finally have a family of her own.

In this next section of Genesis 38, Tamar decides to correct her situation by taking matters into her own hands. As we read about her plan we can identify with her sense of powerlessness. And though we cannot justify her trickery and lies to force Judah to keep his promise to her, this is exactly where God's grace is revealed in her life.

There is an expression that seems appropriate at this point, "There but for the grace of God go I." Without His grace, I could become just like Tamar, operating in my flesh and not walking in the Spirit of God, not seeking God but devising my own way out of tough situations. I have lied, been deceitful, and tried to manipulate people and circumstances for my desired outcome. But when I repent of my actions, God's grace always brings me back to His loving arms by granting me forgiveness as I look to Yeshua, the author and finisher of my faith. (Hebrews 12:1–2)

Consider Tamar's plan and how God's grace was revealed in her life. Instead of sinking back into the evil Canaanite society and living a life of oblivion in her father's home, Tamar seeks her own remedy to the situation. Besides the custom of the "next-in-line brother" raising up seed to provide for a widow, there was another option for continuing the line of the deceased husband through the father-in-law. By this time Judah's wife was dead. It might have seemed logical to Tamar that this would be her ticket to force Judah to fulfill his promise to his daughter-in-law.

She seized the opportunity of the upcoming sheep shearing celebration. She knew that Judah would attend the event and it would be a time when the widower would be lonely and vulnerable.

Her Plot Thickens

On his way to his sheep shearing, Judah's path would take him past one of the Canaanite temples where prostitution was a common religious practice. Disguising herself as a temple prostitute, Tamar placed herself in front of the temple to lure Judah into her trap. As part of the payment, Judah agreed to send a goat through a friend who would deliver it later that day. Tamar shrewdly insisted that Judah provide three items as a security deposit which would identify him and ensure she would be paid.

The three items Tamar requested were his signet ring, his cord/jewelry and his staff—all confirming Judah's identity. The signet ring represented Judah's authority and would carry his seal for signing legal documents. The cord or gold bracelets was a sign of Judah's wealth. The shepherd's staff, most probably carved with his identifying symbols, signified his work in the community. Judah deposits these with Tamar as security for the delivery of the promised sheep, and Tamar returns to her father's home and changes back into her widow's garments.

From Betrayal to Righteousness

Fast forward three months, and Tamar's baby bump is beginning to show. She can no longer hide her pregnancy under her widow's clothing. When Judah Is informed that "she had played the harlot," he responds with anger and condemnation and declares, "Bring her out and let her be burned!" At the conclusion of Judah's self-righteous and judgmental rant Tamar pulls out the three items that belonged to him.

> Now it was about three months later that Judah was informed, "Your daughter-in-law Tamar has played the harlot, and behold, she is also with child by harlotry." Then Judah said, "Bring her out and let her be burned!" It was while she was being brought out that she sent to her father-in-law, saying, "I am with child by the

man to whom these things belong." And she said, "Please examine and see, whose signet ring and cords and staff are these?" And Judah recognized them, and said, "She is more righteous than I, inasmuch as I did not give her to my son Shelah." And he did not have relations with her again. —Genesis 38:24–26

After hearing the full story, Judah declares in front of Tamar and her accusers that she is more righteous than he and confesses that he had betrayed his promise to her. Judah and Tamar never had intercourse again and Tamar did not remarry.

THE LORD IS OUR RIGHTEOUSNESS

The word for "righteous" in Hebrew is *tzadek*, a term used to describe those who follow the LORD and keep His law perfectly. Scripture teaches us that the only One who is truly righteous is the LORD Himself. The prophet Jeremiah prophesied that sometime in the future, a Righteous One from God would become the salvation for Judah:

> "In those days and at that time I will cause a righteous Branch of David to spring forth; and He shall execute justice and righteousness on the earth. In those days Judah shall be saved, and Jerusalem shall dwell in safety; and this is the name by which she shall be called: the LORD is our righteousness—*Adonai Tzidkeynu*." —Jeremiah 33:15, 16

But in the context of the story of Tamar and Judah, how could Tamar be seen as righteous? She had lied and carried out a plan of deceit. This raises the question: How are any of us declared righteous? The Scriptures are clear not only for Tamar and Judah but also for all of us: It is written, "There is none righteous, not even one." (Romans 3:10)

Here again, we find the grace of God continually poured out to us through The Lord our Righteousness. God blesses Tamar with twin sons. Additionally, Tamar, along with her one son, Peretz, are embraced by the family of Judah and become part of his royal line. No longer is Tamar dressed in her widow's garments. As Isaiah says: when we place our trust in the God of Israel we receive new clothes of salvation and righteousness.

> I will rejoice greatly in the LORD, My soul will exult in my God; For He has clothed me with garments of salvation, He has wrapped

me with a robe of righteousness, As a bridegroom decks himself with a garland, And as a bride adorns herself with her jewels.
— Isaiah 61:10

Tamar could rejoice like King David in the psalms, praising God for what he alone could do. God turned her mourning into joy.

"Hear, O Lord, and be gracious to me; O Lord, be Thou my helper. Thou hast turned for me my mourning into dancing; Thou hast loosed my sackcloth and girded me with gladness; That my soul may sing praise to Thee, and not be silent. O Lord my God, I will give thanks to Thee forever." —Psalm 30:10–12

What's in a Name?

The name Tamar in Hebrew means palm tree. We aren't told why Tamar's parents gave her this name but it seems fitting in light of what Judah said about her when he confessed his betrayal of her trust. Was God thinking about Tamar and her situation? It seems evident that God redeemed her situation and gave her peace and posterity. Her name reflected God's accomplishment in her life: those who trust in the Lord will be righteous as the palm tree (tamar) and fruitful even in their old age.

This psalm, which is sung every Sabbath, begins with the declaration.

It is good to give thanks to the Lord, And to sing praises to Thy name, O Most High; to declare Thy lovingkindness in the morning, and Thy faithfulness by night, with the ten-stringed lute, and with the harp; with resounding music upon the lyre. For Thou, O Lord, hast made me glad by what Thou hast done, I will sing for joy at the works of Thy hands. How great are Thy works, O Lord! Thy thoughts are very deep. —Psalm 92:1–5

Note in verse 5 that the Psalmist gives praise for the Lord's greatness as well as His thoughts which are very deep. This is the same word used in Jeremiah 29:11 to describe the plans (thoughts) that God has for you. In God's sovereign plan, He also keeps His promises to Israel. When Jeremiah was writing his 29th chapter, he was speaking to a nation in Babylonian captivity. God is always true to His Word and Jeremiah 29 verse 12–14 reiterate God's faithfulness to Israel and you.

"Then you will call upon Me and come and pray to Me, and I will listen to you. And you will seek Me and find Me, when you search for Me with all your heart. And I will be found by you," declares the LORD, "and I will restore your fortunes and will gather you from all the nations and from all the places where I have driven you," declares the LORD, "and I will bring you back to the place from where I sent you into exile."—Jeremiah 29:12–14

I believe that these promises to Israel from the prophet Jeremiah apply to each of us. Even though Tamar did not know exactly how to seek the God of Israel, the Lord was seeking for her and drawing her to Himself. In her captivity of mourning and despair, God answered Tamar. Did she deserve His grace? Do any of us? Of course not! For God's grace is a gift we neither deserve nor earn. In His grace, God gave Tamar the desire of her heart beyond what she could even ask or imagine. Not only was she included in the family of God, but she and her son are recorded in the royal line of Messiah. She fulfilled her name as a righteous palm tree—*Tzaddik Katamar*—and she honored the LORD in the raising of her sons.

> The righteous will flourish like a palm tree, they will grow like a cedar in the Lebanon. —Psalm 92:13 (CJB)

Perhaps Tamar had been crying out to the God of Judah to understand how her life could be redeemed. Without husband or children, she was reminded of her situation through the widow's garments she was forced to wear in her father's house. God does not justify Tamar's actions, nevertheless, in His abundant merciful compassion He restored her life. Her clothes of mourning became garments of praise. God saw her in grief, despair and disappointment and gave her dignity, hope, and a future. In spite of her deceptive tactics, sleeping with Judah yielded new life. Widowed twice, now God gave her two sons, answering the need of her heart and revealing Himself to her. This is what God wants to do for you and me.

The psalm continues, saying that those who flourish like a Righteous Palm will yield fruit for a long time:

> They will still yield fruit in old age; they shall be full of sap and very green, to declare that the LORD is upright; He is my rock, and there is no unrighteousness in Him. —Psalm 92:14, 15

COMPASSION *and* REDEMPTION

God sees the heart and need of every person, and His desire is for each of us to understand His great love for us. The life of Tamar is a wonderful illustration of how God is concerned for every individual. There are no "throw-away people" in His plan. Even a woman from a condemned pagan culture factored into God's perfect plan.

A Promise for Each of Us
Jeremiah reminds us that God has plans of peace and hope. Could this promise be true for Tamar, a woman with few options, a woman who wore widow's garments and lived in her father's home; betrayed and discounted by her father-in-law Judah, hopeless of enjoying a family of her own? God's plans would overcome Judah's broken promises and God's grace-filled future would override her own desperate trickery and deceit.

> "For I know the plans that I have for you," declares the LORD, "plans for welfare (peace) and not for calamity to give you a future and a hope. Then you will call upon Me and come and pray to Me, and I will listen to you. And you will seek Me and find Me, when you search for Me with all your heart." —Jeremiah 29:11–13

Jeremiah wrote these promises to Israel as they were in exile in Babylon. Even in their despair and defeat, God encourages them to hold onto hope. Like the nation of Israel or the woman Tamar, you may feel you are in a dead-end situation. You may be struggling with bitterness toward someone who has betrayed you. Perhaps unforgiveness is rooted deep in your mind and heart. Let's see if these words from Jeremiah can speak not only to the situations of Tamar and Israel but to each of us as well.

Verse 11 begins with "For I know." When God says He knows (*yadah*), it means He intimately knows you. The perfect tense used here means that God has complete and ongoing knowledge of you. In Psalm 139:1–4 the same Hebrew word, *yadah*, emphasizes that fact in The New Living Translation:

> O LORD, you have examined my heart and know (*yadah*) everything about me. You know when I sit down or stand up. You know my thoughts even when I'm far away. You see me when I travel and when I rest at home. You know everything I do. You know what I am going to say even before I say it, LORD. —Psalm 139:1–4 (NLT)

Jeremiah goes on to say that God also knows the plans He has for us. In Hebrew, the word plan "machshavah" means design, thought, idea or purpose. In modern Hebrew, it connotes how we think about something. In other words, God loves you so much, He is always considering how to design His very best plan for your life.

God's plans for you are for peace (shalom) and not for evil. Shalom is a word that connotes wholeness, fullness and contentment. When you put your trust in Yeshua, this shalom is fulfilled in Him since He is the Prince of Peace (Sar Shalom).

> For a child will be born to us, a son will be given to us; And the government will rest on His shoulders; And His name will be called Wonderful Counselor, Mighty God, Eternal Father, Prince of Peace. —Isaiah 9:6

Furthermore, Yeshua declared to His disciples:

> Peace I leave with you; My peace I give to you; not as the world gives, do I give to you. Let not your heart be troubled, nor let it be fearful. —John 14:27

Please consider what Yeshua is saying to us in this verse. He can give us His peace since He is the embodiment of God's shalom, for not only the world but for your life in particular.

Thankfully, we not only have His peace but we also have God's plans for us, which offer us a future. This word "future"—*acharit* in Hebrew—includes, as it did for Tamar, the promise of descendants and posterity.

But there's more! The word "hope" in Hebrew (*tikvah*) captures the idea of eager expectation and anticipation. Hope is solid and sure if you are trusting in the Lord and His promises. This idea of eager hope is seen in the verb form of "wait" as expressed by King David.

> I waited patiently for the LORD; and He inclined to me, and heard my cry. He brought me up out of the pit of destruction, out of the miry clay; And He set my feet upon a rock making my footsteps firm. And He put a new song in my mouth, a song of praise to our God; Many will see and fear, And will trust in the LORD. How blessed is the man who has made the LORD his

COMPASSION *and* REDEMPTION

trust, And has not turned to the proud, nor to those who lapse into falsehood. Many, O LORD my God, are the wonders which Thou hast done, And Thy thoughts toward us; There is none to compare with Thee; If I would declare and speak of them, They would be too numerous to count. —Psalm 40:1–5

Keeping in mind Jeremiah 29:11, consider how God worked out His plan for Tamar and her children. In the next chapter, we will meet Tamar's sons and discover God's great plan for their families. Not simply included in the line of Judah, they will also bless the future generations of Israel.

But before we go further let's pause and consider how the Lord is working in your life. I pray that the thought questions for your further study will deepen your love and understanding of God's plans for you.

Questions, Thoughts and Reflections

1. Can you relate to Tamar who was in a dead-end situation, still clothed in her garments of mourning with no options? Think of how God desires to change your mourning into dancing and give you His joy. Read the following verses and ask God to help heal you of mourning or bitterness that might be the result of a broken heart. Psalm 34:18, Psalm 30: 1–12, Isaiah 61:1–10 and Luke 4:18–19

2. How does the Lord wrap you in His robe of righteousness? Review Isaiah 61:10 and 2 Corinthians 5:17–21. Meditate on these verses and memorize 2 Corinthians 5:21 He (the Father) made Him (Yeshua) who knew no sin to be sin on our behalf, that we might become the righteousness of God in Him.

3. Personalize Jeremiah 29:11 then take time to thank the Lord for the marvelous truth that He thinks about you and has specific plans and provisions for your life.

3. Do You Need a Breakthrough?

In the previous chapter, we noted that God replaced Tamar's clothes of mourning with garments of praise. As we consider how God provided for Tamar, let your heart be blessed and filled with praise for His abundant grace.

Twins Are Born!

I wonder if during her pregnancy Tamar could have imagined that she would give birth to two sons. Since there were no ultrasounds, these twins may have been a total surprise. However, during the delivery the midwife became aware that there were twins coming; and, as we read in Genesis, this midwife had a plan of action to identify the one born first.

> When she went into labor, it became evident that she was going to have twins. As she was in labor, one of them put out his hand; and the midwife took his hand and tied a scarlet thread on it, saying, "This one came out first." But then he withdrew his hand, and his brother came out; so she said, "How did you manage to break out first?" Therefore, he was named *Peretz* [breaking out]. Then out came his brother, with the scarlet thread on his hand, and he was given the name *Zerah* [scarlet]. — Genesis 38:27–30

The midwife saw a tiny hand emerging from the womb and quickly tied a scarlet thread around his wrist to identify the firstborn. Imagine her surprise as this hand withdrew and suddenly his brother broke out and was born first. Because he broke through, he was named Peretz which means "bursting forth" or "breakthrough."

Every birth is a miracle! I know I felt the miracle power of God when I gave birth to my son Joshua in 1977 and then in 1980 to my second son Matthew. But the birth of Peretz and Zerah seems almost simultaneous. How can one baby have his hand out of the birth canal indicating that he was ready to be born only to have his brother burst out first? The miracle births described in Genesis 38 demonstrate the Lord's providential care for Tamar and her sons. Peretz did more than just break out of the womb first, he also broke through the barrenness of Tamar's life of mourning and confinement. Now, God gives her twin sons! But God had more for Tamar. As we are about to find out, God blesses her family so that they are forever remembered in the Scriptures.

COMPASSION *and* REDEMPTION

Tamar's Gracious Legacy

As the history of Israel continues to unfold, we see that Tamar's son, Peretz, has an important place in the book of Ruth. When Boaz announces that he is the Kinsman Redeemer of Ruth, those who were there to witness their marriage also announced blessings over the couple, as described in Ruth chapter 4.

> And all the people who were in the court, and the elders, said, "We are witnesses. May the LORD make the woman who is coming into your home like Rachel and Leah, both of whom built the house of Israel; and may you achieve wealth in Ephrathah and become famous in Bethlehem. Moreover, may your house be like the house of Peretz whom Tamar bore to Judah, through the offspring which the LORD shall give you by this young woman." —Ruth 4: 11–12

The elders and the people of Bethlehem who blessed the couple could have stopped at the mention of Rachel and Leah. However, in this prayer, the house of Peretz and Tamar is added, praying specifically that Ruth's household will be blessed in the same manner as the house of Peretz. Furthermore, when they include Tamar's name, it affirms that she was fully accepted into the family of Israel. What an honor and what a legacy of blessing this reveals about Tamar's son Peretz and his progeny.

With these recordings in the book of Ruth we know that Peretz continued to be not only a breakthrough baby, but a man who would represent the Lord of the Breakthrough. In breaking out of his mother's womb, Peretz becomes a symbol for overcoming. The Lord has a breakthrough for anyone who will trust in Him. When we are born again into the family of God we pass from the fruitless womb of unbelief and break through into a life of fruitfulness and abundance.

Do you need a Breakthrough in your life?

Whether the thing that is holding you back is a habit, a stronghold of sin, a prayer need, a difficult relationship, a job situation, a family struggle or any other obstacle, a breakthrough is available to each of us. As we will learn from the life of King David, needing a breakthrough puts you in good company.

What is a breakthrough? In human terms, a breakthrough is required when an impassable situation or impenetrable difficulty cannot be overcome through one's own efforts. In the spiritual realm, there is no victory to be found in human maneuvering and machinations to defeat the world, the flesh and the Devil. The LORD of the breakthrough is the only one who can ensure victory in every area of our lives.

The Lord provides David with His breakthrough, when he is finally recognized by all of Israel as their anointed king, after being on the run from King Saul for over 10 years.

> Then all the tribes of Israel came to David at Hebron and said, "Behold, we are your bone and your flesh. Previously, when Saul was king over us, you were the one who led Israel out and in. And the LORD said to you, 'You will shepherd My people Israel, and you will be a ruler over Israel.'" So all the elders of Israel came to the king at Hebron, and King David made a covenant with them before the LORD at Hebron; then they anointed David king over Israel. —2 Samuel 5:1–3

What a victorious time it must have been! David is recognized by Israel, and subsequently captures Zion (Jerusalem) from the Jebusites (2 Samuel 5:7). Through it all, God equipped David with all he needed to succeed in his reign.

> David became greater and greater, for the LORD God of hosts was with him. —2 Samuel 5:10

The name for God that Scripture uses here is *Jehovah Tz'vaot*—"God of the heavenly armies." After being anointed King of Israel, David had to wage war against the enemies of his kingdom. David required *Jehovah Tz'vaot* to be with him in battle.

Fearing David's growing power, the Philistines decide to attack, mobilizing their armies and marching to the Valley of Rephaiim, less than a mile away from Jerusalem. Here in this valley, the Philistines arrayed their considerable forces to conquer David and his army.

GOD'S GRACE IS SEEN IN EVERY BREAKTHROUGH

We read that David went down to his stronghold. Some commentators think that this verse refers to the Cave of Adullam while others believe he retreated to the fortified city of Jerusalem. The exact location is not our concern, but rather what David does there.

> Then David inquired of the Lord, saying, "Shall I go up against the Philistines? Will You give them into my hand?" And the Lord said to David, "Go up, for I will certainly give the Philistines into your hand." —2 Samuel 5:19

Acknowledging that he cannot defeat his enemy unless the Lord delivers the victory, David's warfare is preceded by worship and prayer. The following verse gives an account of this quick and decisive battle.

> So David came to *Baal-Peratzim* and defeated them there; and he (David) said, "The Lord has broken through my enemies before me like the breakthrough of waters." Therefore, he named that place *Baal-Peratzim*—The Lord of the Breakthrough. —2 Samuel 5:20

Here we see that God broke the mighty Philistine army in half through the bursting forth of waters, a tsunami from God, whose irresistible force shattered the enemies who would seek to destroy David and the nation of Israel.

To commemorate this victory, David names the location *Baal-Peratzim*, acknowledging God as the source of the breakthrough and triumph. David also wrote about God's faithfulness to escape the traps and snares of the enemy.

> Our soul has escaped as a bird out of the snare of the trapper; the snare is broken and we have escaped. Our help is in the name of the Lord, Who made heaven and earth. —Psalm 124:7, 8

Shabar, the Hebrew word for "broken" used in Psalm 124, is a synonym for *peretz*—the breaker. Both words convey the idea that only God can break through the ranks of our enemies and foil their deceitful traps. How difficult is it to defeat the deceitfulness of our own flesh? Or to break through the impenetrable walls of discouragement through our own strength? As I fight the good fight of faith, I need the Lord of the Breakthrough every day to fight on my behalf as I entrust myself into His hands. He is the only one who can deliver me from the evil snares of the enemy of my soul.

TAMAR

THE ONE WHO GIVES THE BREAKTHROUGH— A MESSIANIC PROPHECY

Another surprising mention of the breaker is found in the Messianic prophecy written by the prophet Micah. Micah was a contemporary of Isaiah and their writings helped paint a picture of the Messiah of Israel and how he would gather the scattered captives of Israel, break their bondage and lead them to triumph as a redeemed people.

The prophecy of Micah is preceded by an explanation of God's witness against Israel for their idolatry, greed, and rebellion, which are laid out as the causes for their dispersion. Nevertheless, God gives them a promise.

> I will surely assemble all of you, Jacob, I will surely gather the remnant of Israel. I will put them together like sheep in the fold; like a flock in the midst of its pasture They will be noisy with men." —Micah 1:12

This verse assures Israel's restoration, the return of His redeemed ones into the place of God's blessing.

WE ARE THE DEPENDENT SHEEP OF HIS HAND

In the Scriptures, the children of God are often pictured as sheep depending on their shepherd.

> We are the people of His pasture and the sheep of His hand.
> —Psalm 95: 7

Yeshua describes Himself as both the door of the sheepfold and the Good Shepherd.

> "I am the door; if anyone enters through Me, he will be saved, and will go in and out and find pasture. The thief comes only to steal and kill and destroy; I came that they may have life, and have it abundantly. I am the good shepherd; the good shepherd lays down His life for the sheep." —John 10:9–10

What a place of safety and security for God's sheep! Micah 2:12 also states that the flock is in the middle of His sheepfold. Messiah assures us of our security if we dwell in His presence.

COMPASSION *and* REDEMPTION

> "My sheep hear My voice, and I know them, and they follow Me; and I give eternal life to them, and they will never perish; and no one will snatch them out of My hand. My Father, who has given them to Me, is greater than all; and no one is able to snatch them out of the Father's hand. I and the Father are one."
>
> —John 10: 27–30

Yeshua Revealed as the Lord of the Breakthrough

Micah 2:13 foretells what the Messiah will do for this remnant.

> The breaker goes up before them; They break out, pass through the gate and go out by it. So their king goes on before them, And the LORD at their head. —Micah 2:13

The rabbinical writings also identify this as a prophecy of Messiah. In the commentary about this portion in Genesis Rabbah 48:10 the rabbis wrote: In the Messianic future, The breaker is gone up, before them...and the Lord at the head of them (Micah 2:13)[1]

Another commentary from Genesis Rabbah 85:14 agrees: This one is greater than all who will make breaches, for from thee will arise [he of whom it is written], The breaker is gone up before them (Micah 2:13).

When Yeshua came as the One who fulfills these prophecies, early in His ministry He revealed His redemptive purposes in His hometown synagogue. Luke describes Yeshua's visit to His hometown synagogue where He quotes from the scroll of Isaiah 61:1–2.

> And He came to Nazareth, where He had been brought up; and as was His custom, He entered the synagogue on the Sabbath, and stood up to read. And the book of the prophet Isaiah was handed to Him. And He opened the book and found the place where it was written, "the Spirit of the Lord is upon me, because He anointed me to preach the gospel to the poor. He has sent me to proclaim release to the captives, and recovery of sight to the blind, to set free those who are oppressed, to proclaim the favorable year of the

---

[1] Genesis Rabba (B'reshith Rabba) is a religious text from Judaism's classical period, probably written between 300 and 500 CE with some later additions. It is a *midrash* comprising a collection of ancient rabbinical homiletical interpretations of the Book of B'reshith (Genesis).

lord." And He closed the book, gave it back to the attendant and sat down; and the eyes of all in the synagogue were fixed on Him. And He began to say to them, "Today this Scripture has been fulfilled in your hearing." —Luke 4:16–21

In this reading of the prophet Isaiah, Yeshua declared Himself to be the Lord of the Breakthrough—*Baal-Peratzim*! Only the Lord of the Breakthrough can release the captives and set free those who are oppressed, held in their dark dungeons and shackles of sin. This is what Yeshua came to do for each of us. The New Covenant confirms these truths repeatedly.

Messiah Yeshua is the Lord of the Breakthrough

In the fullness of time, the Lord of the Breakthrough broke into this world and opened for each full pardon on the basis of His blood atonement. Now each of us can walk boldly into God's presence because of the His finished work. Is there anything in your life that is too difficult for Yeshua the Breaker to break through so that you can experience His healing, comfort and victory?

- Yeshua broke the power of sin to set us free from the prison of its bondage. He continues to break the power of sin as we trust in Him each day.

What the Messiah has freed us for is freedom! Therefore, stand firm, and don't let yourselves be tied up again to a yoke of slavery. —Galatians 5:1 (CJB)

- Yeshua is the path breaker leading us into the Divine Presence of God and as our King He continues to lead us each step of the way.

Yeshua said, "I AM the Way- and the Truth and the Life; no one comes to the Father except through me." —John 14:6 (CJB)

- Yeshua can break open our stony hearts and give us a heart to love Him:

COMPASSION *and* REDEMPTION

"And I shall give them one heart, and shall put a new spirit within them. And I shall take the heart of stone out of their flesh and give them a heart of flesh, that they may walk in My statutes and keep My ordinances, and do them. Then they will be My people, and I shall be their God." —Ezekiel 11:19–20 (NAS)

- Yeshua breaks down the walls between all people. In synagogue life this wall—the *m'chitza*h—separates men from women. Yeshua broke down the barrier separating us from God and from one another.

But now, you who were once far off have been brought near through the shedding of the Messiah's blood. For he himself is our shalom—he has made us both one and has broken down the *m'chitzah* which divided us. —Ephesians 2:13–14 (CJB)

- We remember Yeshua, our Breaker each time we receive *zikkaron*—Communion.

For what I received from the Lord is just what I passed on to you-that the Lord Yeshua, on the night he was betrayed, took bread; and after he had made the *b'rakhah* he broke it and said, "This is my body, which is for you. Do this as a memorial to me."
—I Corinthians 11: 23–24 (CJB)

- Yeshua, the Lion that is from the tribe of Judah, the Root of David, has overcome and He alone is worthy to break the seals of judgment:

Next I saw in the right hand of the One sitting on the throne a scroll with writing on both sides and sealed with seven seals; and I saw a mighty angel proclaiming in a loud voice, "Who is worthy to open the scroll and break its seals?" But no one in heaven, on earth or under the earth was able to open the scroll or look inside it. I cried and cried, because no one was found worthy to open the scroll or look inside it. One of the elders said to me, "Don't cry. Look, the Lion of the tribe of Y'hudah, the Root of David, has won the right to open the scroll and its seven seals." —Revelation 5:1–5 (CJB)

All of these promises are available to us by God's grace as we place our faith in Yeshua as our Messiah and the Lord of our Breakthrough. But first, we must be broken before Him. For only when we are broken and yielded to Yeshua our King, will He heal our brokenness and restore us.

> "Then your light will break out like the dawn, And your recovery will speedily spring forth; And your righteousness will go before you; The glory of the LORD will be your rear guard. Then you will call, and the LORD will answer; You will cry, and He will say, 'Here I am.'" —Isaiah 58:8–9a

QUESTIONS, THOUGHTS AND REFLECTIONS

1. Take time to pray about any areas of your life where you need and desire a breakthrough.

2. Consider what Yeshua, the Lord of your Breakthrough, can do for you in these areas by looking up the verses listed above. Continue to thank Him for His love and power to help you break through the obstacles in your life as you meditate on the various scriptures to understand what Yeshua has done for you.

SECTION TWO

רחב

RAHAB

"and to Salmon
was born Boaz
by Rahab"
Matthew 1:5

COMPASSION *and* REDEMPTION

4. Before the Walls Came Tumbling Down

The second woman mentioned in the genealogy of Matthew is Rahab.

In order to understand how strategic the life of Rahab was to the nation of Israel as they conquered the land of Canaan, let's examine some important events in Israel's history. Before we come to the famous Battle of Jericho, we need to discover how the Israelites arrived there.

Following 400 years of exile, according to God's promises to Abraham, God miraculously redeems the children of Israel from slavery in Egypt (Genesis 15:13), and they march on the dry land across the bed of the Red Sea. Being freed from physical slavery, however, was only the first step in learning how to live as redeemed children of God. There was much to learn, and one key lesson was to understand that the God of Israel was the one true God and to Him alone belonged praise, honor and worship.

During their many months in the desert, the Lord emphasizes Israel's need to trust God and to avoid idolatry. Moses receives the Torah at Mt. Sinai. This is followed by detailed instructions from God on how to build the Tabernacle—a physical dwelling place for God in their midst. Work is completed, and the presence of the Lord is manifested in a pillar of cloud by day and a pillar of fire by night that hovers above the Tabernacle. Despite this visible presence and in spite of having Moses and Aaron guiding them, something was brewing among many of the Israelites that would prevent them from setting foot into the "land flowing with milk and honey." While the Israelites should have been rejoicing and anticipating their entrance into the Promised Land, they are chastised by the Lord for their faithlessness. Consequently, for the next 40 years, the nation of Israel is left to roam the wilderness until all those who had disbelieved God were dead. What exactly happened to warrant such a severe judgment? Because of the importance for all of us to understand what took place, God gives us warnings in Scripture that refer to the very incident that prevented them from entering the land of promise.

After the Israelites had been in the wilderness for 1–1½ years, they arrive at *Kadesh Barnea*. Both King David and the writer of Hebrews reference this catastrophic account. When the Scripture mentions the names *Massah* and *Meribah*, it's helpful to note that both areas were located at *Kadesh Barnea*.

Danger Ahead!

King David gives stern counsel.

> Come, let us worship and bow down; Let us kneel before the Lord our Maker. For He is our God, And we are the people of His pasture, and the sheep of His hand. Today, if you would hear His voice, Do not harden your hearts, as at Meribah, As in the day of Massah in the wilderness; "When your fathers tested Me, they tried Me, though they had seen My work. For forty years I loathed that generation, and said they are a people who err in their heart, and they do not know My ways. Therefore I swore in My anger, truly they shall not enter into My rest."
> —Psalm 95:6–11

The psalmist begins with an invitation to worship the Lord and to acknowledge that He is our Creator. He calls God's children "sheep," and just as sheep are totally dependent on the shepherd for everything, so God's people are completely reliant upon the Good Shepherd for His care and provision. For our study, the warning that follows this passage is vitally important.

When the Scriptures use the word "today," in Psalm 95:7, it is to convey a sense of immediacy to hearken to God's voice. "Listen" or "hear" in Hebrew is Sh'ma, a word which means to listen to God's instructions with the intention of obeying. The Sh'ma is one of the most well-known prayers in Judaism and is recited in daily prayers as well as each Sabbath in synagogues worldwide. The Sh'ma is from Deuteronomy 6: 4 "Hear, O Israel! The Lord is our God; the Lord is one!"

The Sh'ma is followed by instructions from God as to how we are to obey what He is saying. He gives us a plan to show us how to love the Lord with all our heart, soul and might. The passage with these instructions are called the V'ahavta in Hebrew meaning, "you shall love."

> "And you shall love the Lord your God with all your heart and with all your soul and with all your might. And these words, which I am commanding you today, shall be on your heart; and you shall teach them diligently to your sons and shall talk of them when you sit in your house and when you walk by the way and when you lie down and when you rise up. And you shall bind them as a sign on your hand and they shall be as frontals on your forehead. And you shall write them on the doorposts of your house and on your gates." —Deuteronomy 6:5–9

COMPASSION *and* REDEMPTION

In Deuteronomy 6, God gives us instructions to take His Word into our hearts and live accordingly. In Psalm 95, David gives further instructions by specifically warning us not to harden our hearts like the children of Israel.

What does it mean to be hard-hearted? Consider these few synonyms: unfeeling, insensitive, unresponsive, callous and selfish. Conversely, the antonyms would be: soft-hearted, sensitive, feeling, responsive, kind, vulnerable and teachable.

As we study Numbers 13 and 14, we find the hearts of the Israelites growing hardened and hopefully find a warning that we can apply to our own hearts.

In Numbers 13:32–33, we read of the ten scouts who, after spying out the land, came back with a report that was factual yet very negative. They claimed that the land was rich and productive, yet they recommended against an attempt to conquer it. Excavations show the report to be in full agreement with the facts: Canaan at the time in question was densely populated and blanketed with well-fortified cities.

What caused the ten spies to give such a report? We will discover that they perceived the obstacle through carnal eyes alone. Instead of seeking God's wisdom and taking time to remember the miracles He had already accomplished on their behalf, they ignored the past and saw their future as one of limitations. From the early days of Moses' leadership, God had manifested Himself among them. Yet they forgot the comfort and care of God's presence and His unlimited power, which had already been sufficient in overcoming their past difficulties.

Nothing is Impossible with God

In various seasons of our lives, we have times when our situations may be terrible, miserable, confusing, overwhelming, and seemingly impossible. You or your spouse may be facing a layoff, your health may be in the process of deteriorating, your marriage may be crumbling or you may find yourself estranged from your children. The facts may be painful and frightening. Yet, if we are daughters of the King, we can trust that our all-knowing, all-powerful God cares for us, and that nothing is impossible with Him.

Caleb the Kenizzite along with Joshua, son of Nun, were the only two voices to speak on behalf of God's power to give the Israelites the Promised Land.

Then Caleb quieted the people before Moses, and said, "We should by all means go up and take possession of it, for we shall surely overcome it." —Numbers 13:30

By contrast the other ten spies promoted a different viewpoint:

But the men who had gone up with him said, "We are not able to go up against the people, for they are too strong for us." —Numbers 13:31

The ten fearful spies concluded that the situation was impossible, even for God. Their report disregards the LORD's promise to displace the Canaanites and give Israel the land.

They elaborate, as their bad report takes an almost comical turn:

"It is a land that devours its inhabitants; and all the people whom we saw in it are men of great size." —Numbers 13:32b

This statement seems to contradict itself because if all the people were so large why would they need to devour each other? And if they devour each other, then it seems like it wouldn't be too long a time until all of them were devoured and none would be left!

The word for "bad" in Hebrew is *dibbah*, which carries the meaning of spreading a rumor, or whisper, to defame and give an evil account. How did the children of Israel receive this exaggerated report? Instead of asking God for wisdom, they side with the majority of spies, disregard the minority report and ignore Caleb's exhortation.

LORD, DON'T YOU CARE?

The children of Israel believed the ten faithless spies. They accept their report even though it contradicts the promises that God delivered to the people through Moses and Aaron.

Then all the congregation lifted up their voices and cried, and the people wept that night. —Numbers 14:1

This is like a child not getting her way, crying to show just how upset she is. The child's hope is that her parents will adjust the situation to suit her liking. Many parents recognize "crocodile tears" which are meant to

COMPASSION *and* REDEMPTION

manipulate, and distort the gift of tears our heavenly Father bestowed upon us to enable us to pour out our hearts to Him.

IN TEARS, HANNAH POURS OUT HER SOUL TO THE LORD

When Hannah was distressed because of her childlessness and the cruel tormenting of her rival, Hannah weeps real tears of disappointment, rejection and humiliation.

> ...and she, greatly distressed, prayed to the LORD and wept bitterly. Hannah's tears were real as she sought the LORD. —1 Samuel 1:10

Even when Eli, the priest, falsely accused her of being drunk, she let him know that she was crying to the LORD of Israel.

> But Hannah answered and said, "No, my lord, I am a woman oppressed in spirit; I have drunk neither wine nor strong drink, but I have poured out my soul before the LORD." —1 Samuel 1:15

Do we pour out our hearts to the LORD asking for His comfort, mercy and power to alleviate our pain? Or are we like the Israelites whose tears were shed to manipulate the situation? I know that these tears were not pleasing to God for they were the result of not trusting. Not only is this kind of crying grievous to the Lord but it also promotes grumbling and complaining.

THE GRASS WAS GREENER IN EGYPT

> And all the sons of Israel grumbled against Moses and Aaron: and the whole congregation said to them, "Would that we had died in the land of Egypt! Or would that we had died in this wilderness."
> —Numbers 14:2

Rising up against the leadership of Moses and Aaron, the congregation of Israel makes the ludicrous statement that they would like to return to Egypt, preferring the past to the present. We can laugh at their short memories and their immaturity, but don't we sometimes behave the same way? We don't like the way a situation is unfolding, so we entertain absurd thoughts like the following:

"If only I had stayed with my ungodly boyfriend, OK, he treated me like dirt but at least I would have a date for Saturday night and I wouldn't feel so lonely." Complete this sentence for your own life as you think about the "good old days."

If only I had…

It is possible to indulge in the "grass is always greener" syndrome, turning the past into some sort of idol, longing for the "good old days" when those days were really not that good. The Scriptures exhort us to press on to the high calling in our Messiah Yeshua.

> Therefore, since we have so great a cloud of witnesses surrounding us, let us also lay aside every encumbrance, and the sin which so easily entangles us, and let us run with endurance the race that is set before us, fixing our eyes on Yeshua, the author and perfecter of faith, who for the joy set before Him endured the cross, despising the shame, and has sat down at the right hand of the throne of God.
> —Hebrews 12:1–2

Longing for the past is like driving a car using only the rearview mirror to navigate. How dangerous that would be and what a skewed perspective it would give you! We need to keep our focus on what is ahead of us and only use our rearview mirror to check and gain perspective.

But the children of Israel had a problem; whenever they ran across an obstacle, they longed for the days of their bondage in Egypt. As a result, their faithlessness netted them even more time in the wilderness. What was the source of their constant grumbling and murmuring? They allowed their fears to drive their response. Instead of trusting in God's goodness to them, they questioned His care and provision.

Can I Really Trust You?

They continued their accusations against Moses and God.

> And why is the Lord bringing us into this land, to fall by the sword? Our wives and our little ones will become plunder; would it not be better for us to return to Egypt?   —Numbers 14:3

Their questions revealed the heart of the matter, blaming God for sentencing them and their children to die at the hands of these overwhelming enemy nations? They had reverted to their old whining ways, when they had turned on Moses just before God parted the Red Sea.

COMPASSION *and* REDEMPTION

> "Is this not the word that we spoke to you in Egypt, saying, 'Leave us alone that we may serve the Egyptians? For it would have been better for us to serve the Egyptians than to die in the wilderness.'" —Exodus 14:12

God gave Moses the appropriate response in the following verses:

> But Moses said to the people, "Do not fear! Stand by and see the salvation of the LORD which He will accomplish for you today; for the Egyptians whom you have seen today, you will never see them again forever. The LORD will fight for you while you keep silent." Then the LORD said to Moses, "Why are you crying out to Me? Tell the sons of Israel to go forward. And as for you, lift up your staff and stretch out your hand over the sea and divide it, and the sons of Israel shall go through the midst of the sea on dry land." —Exodus 14:12–16

God told them not to be afraid! That this day would reveal the salvation of the Lord! After the waters parted this was the scene of God's triumph over Egypt:

> The waters returned and covered the chariots and the horsemen, even Pharaoh's entire army that had gone into the sea after them; not one remained. But the sons of Israel walked on dry land through the midst of the sea, and the waters were like a wall to them on their right hand and on their left. Thus the LORD saved Israel that day from the hand of the Egyptians, and Israel saw the Egyptians dead on the seashore. And when Israel saw the great power which the LORD had used against the Egyptians, the people feared the LORD, and they believed in the LORD and in His servant Moses. —Exodus 14:28–31

Now, just one year later, almost all the children of Israel, led by their fears, believed the bad report of something that they believe was too hard for their God. Their fear and unbelief led to outright rebellion against the leader God had appointed.

> So they said to one another, "Let us appoint a leader and return to Egypt." —Numbers 14:4

RAHAB

Do I Ever Respond Like the Israelites?
Before we judge the ten spies too harshly, it will be helpful for our own understanding to review how the children of Israel arrived at this place of rebellion and disbelief. In First Corinthians 10 we are reminded that what happened to Israel in the wilderness was written down for our benefit so that we can learn from their mistakes.

> Now these things happened to them as an example, and they were written for our instruction, upon whom the ends of the ages have come. Therefore let him who thinks he stands take heed lest he fall. —1 Corinthians 10:11–12 (NAS)

Let's take a moment to see if we have fallen into any of this behavior. Ask yourself these questions with me to evaluate if our first response is one of fear or of faith.

1. In an overwhelming situation is my first response to start crying to try to manipulate God to get my own way? I know that I can murmur and grumble if I don't agree with how I perceive God is working things out. I can easily fall back into thinking that God doesn't really understand all the facts. Instead of trusting, I complain.

2. Have I given into fear about the future allowing worry to dominate my response? Even though I desire for faith to be my first response, I often permit a reaction of fear to override my best intentions.

3. Where does fear lead me? If I am not vigilant, fear can surface as accusations against God followed by rebellion or even rejection of His authority.

The Minority Report—Believing God
Poised on the brink of entering the Promised Land, there was a godly remnant represented by Moses, Aaron, Joshua and Caleb whose response to the despicable behavior of the children of Israel was to throw themselves upon the mercy of God:

COMPASSION *and* REDEMPTION

> Then Moses and Aaron fell on their faces in the presence of the assembly of the congregation of the sons of Israel. —Numbers 14:5

The Hebrew for "fall" is *naphal,* which means to throw oneself down, humbling oneself before God and, in this case, in front of the entire congregation. Joshua and Caleb tore their clothes, a sign of mourning and repentance as they continued to plead with the people to believe God and not the report of the faithless spies.

> And Joshua the son of Nun and Caleb the son of Jephunneh, of those who had spied out the land, tore their clothes; and spoke to all the congregation of the sons of Israel, saying, "The land which we passed through to spy out is an exceedingly good land. "If the Lord is pleased with us, then He will bring us into this land, and give it to us—a land which flows with milk and honey."Only do not rebel against the Lord; and do not fear the people of the land, for they shall be our prey. Their protection has been removed from them, and the Lord is with us; do not fear them." —Numbers 14:6–9

How does Joshua describe the land? He calls it "exceedingly good." The Hebrew phrase is *tov me'od* and it expresses a superlative degree of goodness. More important, what does Joshua say about the Lord? Joshua gives the children of Israel a conditional promise. If they do something, then God will respond in a certain way. If they do not rebel but rather do what pleases God by trusting in His promises, then they will have nothing to fear. What Joshua declares is that God has removed the enemy's protection. This Hebrew word for "protection" means shadow or shelter—expressing the transitory nature of life. When the Lord is with us in this godless world we need not fear because He is our protection! Nevertheless, we must always be careful not to harden our hearts.

Joshua's exhortation reminds me of the time David escaped from the King of Gath and from the Philistines who would have surely killed him.

> When I am afraid, I will put my trust in Thee. In God, whose word I praise, In God I have put my trust; I shall not be afraid. What can mere man do to me? David repeats his trust in the Lord later in the Psalm: Then my enemies will turn back in the day when I call; This I know, that God is for me. In God, whose

word I praise, In the LORD, whose word I praise, In God I have put my trust, I shall not be afraid. What can man do to me?
—Psalm 56:3–11

I have tried to memorize these essential verses. When I am afraid they remind me to trust the LORD. If God is for us, then who can stand against us?

Sadly, the children of Israel did not change their minds about taking the land. Because they hardened their hearts, they were sentenced to wander for the next 38 years until each one had perished in the wilderness. In a sense, God gave them exactly what they wanted.

In the next chapter, we will enter the Promised Land with Joshua and meet one of my heroines of the faith, Rahab!

QUESTIONS, THOUGHTS AND REFLECTIONS:
1. The warning found in Psalm 95 is repeated in Hebrews 3:7–11 and in Hebrews 3:15. Read all these Scriptures and consider what makes this warning so valuable for us today. Do we allow our hearts to grow cold and hard?

Therefore, as the Ruach HaKodesh says, "Today, if you hear God's voice, don't harden your hearts, as you did in the Bitter Quarrel on that day in the Wilderness when you put God to the test. Yes, your fathers put me to the test; they challenged me, and they saw my work for forty years! Therefore, I was disgusted with that generation and said, 'Their hearts are always going astray, they have not understood how I do things'; in my anger, I swore that they would not enter my rest." Watch out, brothers, so that there will not be in any one of you an evil heart lacking trust, which could lead you to apostatize from the living God! Instead, keep exhorting each other every day, as long as it is called Today, so that none of you will become hardened by the deceit of sin. For we have become sharers in the Messiah, provided, however, that we hold firmly to the conviction we began with, right through until the goal is reached. Now where it says, "Today, if you hear God's voice, don't harden your hearts, as you did in the Bitter Quarrel," who were the people who, after they heard, quarreled so bitterly? All those whom Moshe brought out of Egypt. And with whom was God disgusted for forty years? Those who sinned—yes, they fell dead in the Wilderness! And to whom was it that he swore that they would not enter his rest? Those who were disobedient. So we see that they were unable to enter because of lack of trust.

—Hebrews 3:7 (CJB)

2. Think about your life and if you have any areas where you are resenting how God allowed things to turn out. Confess to the LORD any "grass is greener on the other side" attitudes that may be hindering your walk with Him.

RAHAB

5. From Harlot to Heroine

In our glimpse of the historical setting of Rahab's story, we noted that the children of Israel's entrance to the land of milk and honey was put on hold for 40 years. Now that the generation who disbelieved God's promises were gone, the time had finally arrived to take the land. After the death of Moses, God chose Joshua, son of Nun, to lead the Israelites. The Lord commissioned Joshua to conquer Canaan with His guidance, offering assurance of His presence throughout the process.

> God said to Joshua, "Have I not commanded you? Be strong and courageous! Do not tremble or be dismayed, for the LORD your God is with you wherever you go."   —Joshua 1:9

When Joshua assumed command, the children of Israel promise obedience and loyalty.

> "Just as we obeyed Moses in all things, so we will obey you: only may the LORD your God be with you, as He was with Moses."
> —Joshua 1: 17

What a dramatic change from the generation before when all of Israel rebelled against not only their leaders but also against the LORD!

Joshua's plan, as they approached the land, was to send two spies into the walled city of Jericho and gather intelligence. In Hebrew, the word "view" or "spy out" is the commonly used ra'ah or "see." Ra'ah carries the idea of evaluating and advising in light of what is seen. Because Joshua trusted that God would deliver the land into their hands, he knew that the spies would be protected and guided. He wanted to be wise both in his planning and in his approach of the city.

This is when we first meet Rahab.

> Then Joshua the son of Nun sent two men as spies secretly from Shittim, saying, "Go, view the land, especially Jericho." So they went and came into the house of a harlot whose name was Rahab, and lodged there.   —Joshua 2:1

Providence—God's Hand in the Glove of History

A quick read of this verse immediately raises questions. How did the two spies make their way into the city without being recognized as strangers? How did they meet Rahab, and why did they go into a house of prostitution? The answer is that God knew Rahab's heart was turning to Him.

This unfolding drama offers a demonstration of the providence of God who led the spies to the only believing home in Jericho. However, the spies were quickly recognized when the king of Jericho sent his men to confront Rahab. Rahab knew that these spies would lose their lives if she revealed that they were in her home. The Canaanites were sworn enemies of Israel and sought to defeat them and their God. Now that she had turned to the God of Israel, God gave her His grace. She hid the spies on her rooftop, gave the king's men false intelligence, and diverted their attention away from her home.

Rahab's Faith in the One True God

Rahab's faith is described as she talks to the spies.

> And (Rahab) said to the men, "I know that the LORD has given you the land, and that the terror of you has fallen on us, and that all the inhabitants of the land have melted away before you. For we have heard how the LORD dried up the water of the Red Sea before you when you came out of Egypt, and what you did to the two kings of the Amorites who were beyond the Jordan, to Sihon and Og, whom you utterly destroyed." — Joshua 2:9–10

Rahab begins by saying that she knew God would be victorious and keep His promises to His people. She also understood that Jericho was a doomed city. She had heard of the miracle of the Red Sea and the defeat of the two powerful kings on the other side of the Jordan River and these facts travelled from her head to her heart, turning into faith and trust. Everyone in Jericho heard the same accounts and responded in terror, except Rahab. Verse 11 states that the people had no ruach, the Hebrew word for breath, wind or spirit. In this case it is translated "courage." For Rahab, fear of the Lord translated into reverence and awe.

> "And when we heard it, our hearts melted and no courage remained in any man any longer because of you; for the LORD your God, He is God in heaven above and on earth beneath."
>
> —Joshua 2:11

RAHAB

Rahab's affirmation here and in verses 9 and 10, reveals that she had already trusted in the God of Israel. I think it bears repeating: when Joshua told the scouts to go "see" the land, Joshua knew that these spies were not alone in their reconnaissance mission. Joshua knew that the same God who provided a ram for Abraham's sacrifice is the same God who sees and provides a way for His servants to "see" as well. The name "God Will Provide"—*Jehovah Yireh*—comes from the binding of Isaac in Genesis 22:14 and literally means "the LORD who sees." In other words, God sees the need and provides accordingly. God saw ahead in the life of Rahab and provided a home on the walls of Jericho as a safe haven not only for the spies but also for her family in the midst of wartime and terror. Rahab was the only person in Jericho who trusted the God of Israel, and that same God led the spies straight to her door.

RAHAB—HARLOT OR HEROINE?

Some Jewish scholars and Christian teachers insist that Rahab was not really a harlot, but an innkeeper. However, when Rahab is introduced in Joshua 2:1 and later in Joshua 6:25, the Hebrew word, *zanah*, is repeated which means "one who practices prostitution." The New Covenant confirms this label. In both James 2:25 and Hebrews 11:31, the writers use the Greek word, *porne*, (root of the word "pornography," also translated "prostitute") to describe Rahab. Could it be that by the time the spies came to her home, because of her faith in the God of Israel, she may have been using her location as an inn rather than a house of prostitution? Perhaps. One thing is certain, Rahab's label as a harlot did not define her in the Lord's eyes, for He chose to use her in an extraordinary way to accomplish His purposes. By her courageous faith and works, she is forever recorded in the Hall of Faith in Hebrews 11, named right alongside Noah, Abraham, Moses and Joseph. Only three women are mentioned there: Sarah (Hebrews 11:11), Moses's parents that included his mother Jochebed (11:23), and Rahab the harlot (11:31).

> By faith Rahab the harlot did not perish along with those who were disobedient, after she had welcomed the spies in peace.
> —Hebrews 11:31

James uses Rahab as an example of someone who didn't just claim to believe but who demonstrated that trust in a tangible way.

COMPASSION *and* REDEMPTION

> In the same way was not Rahab the harlot also justified by works, when she received the messengers and sent them out by another way?
> —James 2:25

But why would the New Covenant keep the label of harlot? According to 2 Corinthians 5:17, any person who accepts Messiah Yeshua as Lord and Savior is a new creation. Could this former label be God showing us His unending grace in the life of Rahab? In Messiah, we are no longer defined by our old labels, yet remembering where we came from can give cause for rejoicing and thanksgiving for where He has brought us. God changed Rahab and used her mightily to assure victory for Israel. She was no longer Rahab the harlot, but rather she was Rahab, a daughter of the God of Israel. She is a heroine of our faith, an example of God's abundant mercy to change and redeem. Let's discover how God saved her life and the lives of her entire household.

A Deeper Look at Rahab's Faith

Just as God had worked out all things for good in the life of Tamar, He grants favor and wisdom to Rahab and answers the longings of her heart. As we take a closer look at Rahab's plea to the spies, we will see how God reveals Himself. God loved Rahab, and even though she lived in one of the most notoriously pagan and well-fortified cities in the land, nothing could stop His eternal love from reaching her heart.

Rahab's appeal to the spies uses several words that give us a glimpse into Rahab's faith.

> "Now therefore, please swear to me by the LORD, since I have dealt kindly with you, that you also will deal kindly with my father's household, and give me a pledge of truth, and spare my father and my mother and my brothers and my sisters, with all who belong to them, and deliver our lives from death."
> —Joshua 2:12–13

Rahab's choice of words reveals several key attributes of her faith. She asks them, "swear to me by the LORD." The Hebrew word for "swear" is shava, the root of the word shavuah, meaning "week" or "vow." It is also connected to sheva, or "seven," the number of completeness. The word "swear" implies total faithfulness in the fulfilling of a vow.

Furthermore, Rahab tells the spies to swear the oath using the covenant name of the Lord, the Hebrew letters *yud, hey, vav, hey*. This is the name that God revealed to His servant Moses from the burning bush. God tells Moses to lead the children of Israel out of the land of Egypt and Moses objects:

> Behold, I am going to the sons of Israel, and I shall say to them, "The God of your fathers has sent me to you." Now they may say to me, "What is His name?" What shall I say to them?
> —Exodus 3:13

In response, God reveals His Covenant Name to Moses—

> And God said to Moses, "I Am Who I Am"; and He said, "Thus you shall say to the sons of Israel, 'I Am has sent me to you.'"
> —Exodus 3:14

Because Rahab had heard of what the God of Israel had done for His people, to deliver them from the Egyptians, it was important to her that they guaranteed their promise by the Name of their God.

I love that Rahab repeats the word "kindly" two times. She requests that the spies deal kindly with her and her household. Kindly is *chesed* in Hebrew, a word which usually refers to God's covenant love for us. Rahab cares for those she loves as she asks for deliverance for her family, specifically mentioning her father, her mother, her sisters, her brothers and all who belong to them.

One of my favorite verses that describes God's chesed, His covenant love, is found in Jeremiah.

> The Lord appeared to him from afar, saying, "I have loved you with an everlasting love; Therefore I have drawn you with lovingkindness (*chesed*).
> —Jeremiah 31:3

A Miracle Sign is Needed

At the end of Joshua 2:12, Rahab also asks for a pledge or sign of truth. "Sign" is *ot* in Hebrew and is usually translated as a "miracle sign." A familiar example is found in Exodus where the word is used for the blood of the Lamb on the doors in Egypt.

> And the blood shall be a sign (*ot*) for you on the houses where you live; and when I see the blood I will pass over you, and no plague will befall you to destroy you when I strike the land of Egypt.
> —Exodus 12:13

Another example of the use of miracle sign is in the prophecy of the virgin birth.

> Therefore the Lord Himself will give you a sign (*ot*); "Behold, a virgin will be with child and bear a son, and she will call His name Immanuel." —Isaiah 7:14

Hearing with Faith to Obey

How did Rahab have this knowledge of the God of Israel? The key to understanding her faith is found in Joshua 2:11 when she tells the spies, "And when we heard it, our hearts melted and no courage remained in any man any longer because of you; for the LORD your God, He is God in heaven above and on earth beneath." We noted before that the Hebrew word for "heard" is Sh'ma which implies listening not merely with intellectual understanding but with the intent of obedience. Everyone heard the same stories of the miracles of God, but only Rahab opened her heart to listen and believe.

Rahab's Miracle Sign—The Scarlet Cord of Hope

The sign of Rahab's deliverance was a scarlet cord that the spies instructed her to hang from her window on the wall facing the direction of those coming to conquer Jericho.

> The men said to her, "We shall be free from this oath to you which you have made us swear, unless, when we come into the land, you tie this cord of scarlet thread in the window through which you let us down, and gather to yourself into the house your father and your mother and your brothers and all your father's household."
> —Joshua 2:17–18

This scarlet cord cannot be overlooked. This sign foreshadows the redemption God would ultimately provide in Yeshua the Messiah. This shade of red is the color of the blood that was shed for each of us. The prophet Isaiah invites sinners with this redemptive invitation:

"Come now, and let us reason together," says the Lord, "Though your sins are as scarlet, they will be as white as snow; though they are red like crimson, they will be like wool. — Isaiah 1:18

Not only is the color significant, but the word for cord is telling. "Cord" in Hebrew is *tikvah*, the word for "hope." In the study of Tamar, we looked at Jeremiah 29:11 where God promises His children "a future and a hope." Hope means confident expectation. When we hope in the Lord, we will not be disappointed. The New Covenant fulfills the hope of our redemption through the Lamb of God who takes away the sin of the world.

Therefore having been justified by faith, we have peace with God through our Lord Yeshua the Messiah, through whom also we have obtained our introduction by faith into this grace in which we stand; and we exult in hope of the glory of God. And not only this, but we also exult in our tribulations, knowing that tribulation brings about perseverance; and perseverance, proven character; and proven character, hope; and hope does not disappoint, because the love of God has been poured out within our hearts through the Holy Spirit who was given to us. —Romans 5:1–5

What a miraculous sign for Rahab! The scarlet cord of confident expectation. Rahab was careful to follow the instructions given by the spies as she waited to be delivered.

"According to your words, so be it." So she sent them away, and they departed; and she tied the scarlet cord in the window. —Joshua 2:21

The Walls Came Tumbling Down

Some of us are familiar with the part of this narrative when Joshua fights the battle of Jericho. I always love teaching this amazing portion to children because it gives me an opportunity to realize over and over again the excitement and drama as the walls of Jericho came tumbling down. This miracle of God's victory over the mighty walled city emphasizes how our powerful God can overcome any obstacle if we trust Him to do it His way. I like teaching the catchy kid's chorus of "Joshua Fit [Fought] the Battle of Jericho," which highlights this astounding miracle.

COMPASSION *and* REDEMPTION

> Joshua fit the battle of Jericho,
> Jericho, Jericho,
> Joshua fit the battle of Jericho,
> And the walls came tumbling down!

One reason that the battle of Jericho is so exciting concerns God's seemingly bizarre battle plan, telling Joshua to have the Israelites march around the city once a day, for six days. The priests were to carry the ark and blow trumpets, but the soldiers were to remain silent. On the seventh day, the assembly would march around the city walls seven times. By God's order, every living thing in the city would be destroyed, except Rahab and her family. Articles of silver, gold, bronze and iron were deposited in the Lord's treasury. At Joshua's command, the men gave a great shout, and Jericho's walls fell flat! The Israelites rushed in and conquered the city.

Once an Outcast but Now Part of God's Family
Rahab's home was untouched by the devastation.

> However, Rahab the harlot and her father's household and all she had, Joshua spared; and she has lived in the midst of Israel to this day, for she hid the messengers whom Joshua sent to spy out Jericho.
> —Joshua 6:25

Rahab continues to live in the midst of Israel and marries Salmon. Many scholars believe Salmon had been one of the two spies she hid on her rooftop. Rahab also became part of the family of Israel.

> ...and to Salmon [and Rahab] was born Boaz. —Ruth 4:21

In our next section we will discover how the life of Boaz prefigured the life of Yeshua.

Questions, Thoughts and Reflections
1. How does Rahab's declaration of her faith in the Lord challenge you? Remember, she had no Scriptures, no personal witness and held a degrading profession in a wicked, idol worshipping society to name a few obstacles.

RAHAB

Read 2 Chronicles 16:9a "For the eyes of the LORD move to and fro throughout the earth that He may strongly support those whose heart is completely His" and consider how this applies to Rahab's life and to your own.

2. Reflect on the danger of allowing old labels to define you. You are not what society calls you. You are who your Heavenly Father says you are: a daughter of the King of kings, an ambassador for Messiah, a servant of the Most High God, an heir and joint heir with Messiah Yeshua, just to name a few aspects of your new identity.

COMPASSION *and* REDEMPTION

6. Do You Need a Hero?

Rahab's son Boaz is a key figure in the touching redemption story of Ruth and Naomi. In the next section about Ruth we will delve further into the role of Boaz. For now, let's examine how the life of Boaz prefigures the Messiah of Israel.

In the book of Ruth, we are introduced to Boaz and learn much about him.

> Now Naomi had a kinsman of her husband, a man of great wealth, of the family of Elimelech, whose name was Boaz.
> —Ruth 2:1

To begin with, Boaz is a kinsman or relative—*modah*—from the Hebrew root *yadah*, "to know." This word tells us that Boaz was a close relative, not a 3rd or 4th cousin, but one who was closely connected to the family of Elimelech.

The next phrase, "a man of great wealth" reveals how the community of Boaz regarded him. Several translations, including the King James, the *Complete Jewish Bible* and the *English Standard Version* offer even further insight in their translations: "a mighty man of wealth" (KJV); "a prominent and wealthy member of the clan" (CJB); "a worthy man" (ESV). These communicate a sense that Boaz was mighty, rich, prominent and well-deserved of his honor and respect in the community who regarded him as a worthy man. The Hebrew *Gibbor Hayil* gives us an even deeper understanding, which points us to the very nature of our Messiah, Yeshua.

I Need a Hero—Yeshua, My Gibbor Hayil

Do you ever find yourself wishing or even praying that a wealthy, well-connected savior would come galloping into your life on his magnificent white horse and rescue you from all your troubles? He would not only settle your credit card debt, but also whisk you away to his castle where the two of you would live happily ever. Do not fear, for your Gibbor Hayil is here. The two-word Hebrew description of Boaz combines *gibbor* (hero or champion) with *hayil*, which indicates great power and wealth.

Psalm 45 adds a prophetic dimension to this Hero of Strength, portraying King Messiah who will vanquish all our enemies.

RAHAB

> Gird your sword on your side, you mighty (gibbor) one; clothe yourself with splendor and majesty. In your majesty ride forth victoriously in the cause of truth, humility and justice; let your right hand achieve awesome deeds. Let your sharp arrows pierce the hearts of the king's enemies; let the nations fall beneath your feet. Your throne, O God, will last for ever and ever; a scepter of justice will be the scepter of your kingdom. You love righteousness and hate wickedness; therefore God, your God, has set you above your companions by anointing you with the oil of joy.
> —Psalm 45:3–7(NIV)

The psalm goes on to explain how our Mighty Hero is the perfect picture of our beloved Messiah. (footnote: If you want to study Psalm 45 more fully you can get the book Eternally Desired or go to www.wordofmessiah.org to view a free video of the teaching on this chapter, Part 1 of the Eternally Desired Video Series)

Rather than just being a Mighty man, Yeshua the Messiah was prophesied to be the *El Gibbor*. This title, meaning "Mighty God" is also found in the prophecy of Isaiah 9:6 where Yeshua's names are listed. These names reflect His character, His boundless strength and His limitless power to deliver each of us.

> For a child will be born to us, a son will be given to us; And the government will rest on His shoulders; And His name will be called Wonderful Counselor, Mighty God, (*El Gibbor*), Eternal Father, Prince of Peace. —Isaiah 9:6

EL GIBBOR'S POWER TO REDEEM

The life of Boaz foreshadows what Yeshua would ultimately fulfill for us as *Goel*, or "Redeemer." As the *goel* of the book of Ruth, Boaz was able and willing to pay the price to redeem the property of Elimelech, marry Ruth and carry on the family name. (Ruth 4:14)

> And Naomi said to her daughter-in-law, "May he be blessed of the LORD who has not withdrawn his kindness to the living and to the dead." Again, Naomi said to her, "The man is our relative, he is one of our closest relatives (*goel*)." —Ruth 2:20

COMPASSION *and* REDEMPTION

The *Complete Jewish Bible* and the *New International Version* translate closest relative first as "our redeeming kinsmen," and then "our guardian-redeemers."

> The man is closely related to us; he's one of our redeeming kinsmen.
> (CJB)

> That man is our close relative; he is one of our guardian-redeemers.
> (NIB)

After Boaz and Ruth are married, the women of Bethlehem pronounce a blessing over Naomi where the word redeemer is used.

> So Boaz took Ruth, and she became his wife, and he went in to her. And the LORD enabled her to conceive, and she gave birth to a son. Then the women said to Naomi, "Blessed is the LORD who has not left you without a redeemer (*goel*) today, and may his name become famous in Israel." —Ruth 4:13

The Lord used a willing and able Boaz to redeem the property and family name of Naomi and fulfill his role as the kinsman redeemer by marrying Ruth. In Yeshua the Messiah we have a perfect fulfillment of all that Boaz foreshadowed. Because of his position as the closest relative or kinsman, Boaz was able to redeem the property of Elimelech and marry Ruth to carry on the family line of Naomi. Yeshua the Messiah is our Kinsman Redeemer, for when He took on human flesh and entered this time space continuum, we were invited back into the family of God to live as His children with all the privileges of a family member. I am listing just a few Scriptures to emphasize the love of Yeshua who became one of us in order to redeem us. I pray that your heart will be overflowing with gratitude and praise to Yeshua as you realize afresh what He has done for you.

> And the Word became flesh, and dwelt among us, and we beheld His glory, glory as of the only begotten from the Father, full of grace and truth. —John 1:14

> But as many as received Him, to them He gave the right to become children of God, even to those who believe in His name. —John 1:12

See how great a love the Father has bestowed upon us, that we should be called children of God; and such we are. For this reason the world does not know us, because it did not know Him. Beloved, now we are children of God, and it has not appeared as yet what we shall be. We know that, when He appears, we shall be like Him, because we shall see Him just as He is.   —1 John 3:1–2

Yeshua the Redeemer Purchased my Redemption

Boaz used his great wealth and resources to buy back the land and redeem what had once been lost to Naomi. Yeshua the Messiah has all the resources of heaven at His disposal and in submission to His Heavenly Father became our Redeemer-Goel. In the Hebrew Scriptures, Messiah Yeshua is called the Redeemer by many including Job, King David, Solomon, Asaph, Isaiah and Jeremiah.

Even in the midst of his sorrows and pain Job assuredly declared: "And as for me, I know that my Redeemer lives, and at the last He will take His stand on the earth."   —Job 19:25

In light of God's creation and His perfect Word, King David prayed that his words and his thoughts would be pleasing to his Rock and his Redeemer:

Let the words of my mouth and the meditation of my heart be acceptable in Thy sight, O Lord, my Rock and my Redeemer.
—Psalm. 19:14

The worship leader, Asaph, spoke about the children of Israel during their wilderness wanderings:

And they remembered that God was their rock, and the Most High God their Redeemer.   —Psalm 78:35

King Solomon wrote of the need to have a strong Redeemer for those who desire to follow God's wisdom in their lives.

For their Redeemer is strong; He will plead their case against you.   —Proverbs. 23:11

COMPASSION *and* REDEMPTION

The prophet Isaiah declares to Israel that the Lord is their Redeemer numerous times; and because the Lord is their Redeemer, they do not have to be afraid.

> But now, thus says the Lord, your Creator, O Jacob, And He who formed you, O Israel, "Do not fear, for I have redeemed you; I have called you by name; you are Mine!" —Isaiah 43:1

> Thus says the Lord, the King of Israel and his Redeemer, the Lord of hosts: "I am the first and I am the last, And there is no God besides Me." —Isaiah 44:6

Yeshua's Redemption Fulfilled in the New Covenant: The Apostle Peter explains our redemption in his first letter.

> Knowing that you were not redeemed with perishable things like silver or gold from your futile way of life inherited from your forefathers, but with precious blood, as of a lamb unblemished and spotless, the blood of Messiah. —1 Peter 1:18, 19

And the Apostle Paul writes about various aspects of our redemption in Yeshua our Redeemer in many of his epistles:

> Messiah redeemed us from the curse of the Law, having become a curse for us, for it is written, "Cursed is everyone who hangs on a tree." —Galatians 3:13

> But when the fulness of the time came, God sent forth His Son, born of a woman, born under the Law, in order that He might redeem those who were under the Law, that we might receive the adoption as sons. And because you are sons, God has sent forth the Spirit of His Son into our hearts, crying, "Abba! Father!" —Galatians 4:4–6

> (He) gave Himself for us, that He might redeem us from every lawless deed and purify for Himself a people for His own possession, zealous for good deeds. —Titus 2:14

In Him we have redemption through His blood, the forgiveness of

our trespasses, according to the riches of His grace, which He lavished upon us. In all wisdom and insight
—Ephesians 1:7–8 (also 1:14, 4:30)

But by His doing you are in Messiah Yeshua, who became to us wisdom from God, and righteousness and sanctification, and redemption, that, just as it is written, "Let him who boasts, boast in the Lord." —1 Corinthians 1:30–31

In the book of Hebrews, the author is clear to highlight our eternal redemption.

And not through the blood of goats and calves, but through His own blood, He entered the holy place once for all, having obtained eternal redemption. For if the blood of goats and bulls and the ashes of a heifer sprinkling those who have been defiled, sanctify for the cleansing of the flesh, how much more will the blood of Messiah, who through the eternal Spirit offered Himself without blemish to God, cleanse your conscience from dead works to serve the living God? And for this reason He is the mediator of a new covenant, in order that since a death has taken place for the redemption of the transgressions that were committed under the first covenant, those who have been called may receive the promise of the eternal inheritance. —Hebrews 9:12–15

This is just a sampling of the many verses which speak of our Redeemer, Yeshua and His work of redemption. Please take time to examine your own heart and consider where you stand with God. Can you say with Job that "I know my Redeemer lives?" If you have accepted Yeshua as your Messiah and Savior, you have a Mighty Hero who loves you with an everlasting love. Yeshua the Messiah became your Kinsman Redeemer and paid the price in full to bring you into God's family and add you to His genealogy of grace. Yeshua is your Redeemer and your Mighty God who will protect you and eternally provide for you. However, if you have not accepted Yeshua as your Messiah and Redeemer ask God to show you the truth of Yeshua and His redemptive power. Consider the amazing love that He has for you and open your heart to Him today.

COMPASSION *and* REDEMPTION

QUESTIONS, THOUGHTS AND REFLECTIONS

1. Read the Scriptures that describe how Yeshua is our Kinsman, our Redeemer and our Mighty God. Go over the verses listed and consider what Yeshua has done for you. Then take time to worship Him with praise and thanksgiving in your heart.

2. Consider some aspects of redemption and write down how Messiah Yeshua fulfills every aspect of redemption in your life. For your own study, consider the following verses where the Lord is declared to be the Redeemer and apply them to your own life: Isaiah 44: 6 and 24, 47:4, 48:17, 59:20, 60:16, 63:16, Jeremiah 50:34

3. Memorize one of the verses in this section that you find most meaningful for your life.

SECTION THREE

רות
RUTH

"and to Boaz
was born Oved
by Ruth"
Matthew 1:5

COMPASSION *and* REDEMPTION

7. A Famine in the House of Bread!

In this section we meet Ruth, the third woman included in Matthew's genealogy. In our previous studies of Tamar and Rahab, we noted that both women were from the accursed nation of the Canaanites. Because of Canaan's wickedness and idolatry, God had condemned the entire nation and demanded that they be wiped out. Nevertheless, we saw in the lives of both Tamar and Rahab that, instead of being destroyed, the grace of God was poured out upon them as they were adopted into God's family and became beloved daughters of the King of kings forever included in the LORD's genealogy of grace.

Ruth was born into the accursed nation of Moab and is often identified as Ruth the Moabite.

> No Ammonite or Moabite shall enter the assembly of the LORD; none of their descendants, even to the tenth generation, shall ever enter the assembly of the LORD, because they did not meet you with food and water on the way when you came out of Egypt, and because they hired against you Balaam the son of Beor from Pethor of Mesopotamia, to curse you. Nevertheless, the LORD your God was not willing to listen to Balaam, but...turned the curse into a blessing for you because the LORD your God loves you. You shall never seek their peace or their prosperity all your days.
> —Deuteronomy 23:3–6

Even though the LORD had cursed the nation of Moab, He included Ruth in the royal line of the Messiah of Israel. We rejoice together as we see God's astounding grace in Ruth's life. Ruth became a vessel of healing to Naomi; and, like Rachel and Leah, Ruth helped build the house of Israel.

An Amazing Honor—Her own book!

Of the five women named in Matthew's genealogy, Ruth is the only woman to have a book of the Bible that bears her name and story. Many scholars believe that Samuel, the prophet of Israel, authored these four chapters. Ruth stands alongside Esther as the only other woman for whom a book from the Hebrew Scriptures is named.

And, standing alone, Ruth is the only Gentile woman to have this honor.

RUTH

Everyone Doing What's Right in His Own Sight!

Each of our studies has noted a progression in the history of Israel. When we met Tamar, the families of Israel were just forming; then, hundreds of years later, we were introduced to Rahab during the conquering of the land that God had promised earlier to the twelve tribes of Israel. After they conquered the nations inhabiting the land, Joshua then assigned the tribes their various portions of the land of Israel. The time that followed, called the period of the Judges, is the historical setting for the book of Ruth.

Unfortunately, during the 300 years of the Judges, there is increasing anarchy and idolatry in Israel—a cycle that is repeated over and over. First, the Israelites would turn to idols. Then their enemies would oppress them. Finally, when the people of Israel became desperate, they would cry out to the Lord. In response, God would raise up a Judge to redeem them. Then the cycle would start over.

These Judges were set in place by God to adjudicate private and public matters and give the Israelites guidance for their everyday lives. However, there was no Israeli Defense Force to make sure their policies were followed. God Himself wanted to be their King to reign over them; but, for the most part, the people rejected the rule of God and His appointed judges as well. Instead, they behaved as is described in the concluding verse of the book of Judges:

> In those days, there was no king in Israel; everyone did what was right in his own eyes. —Judges 21:25

We are assured throughout Scripture that God always maintains a believing and loyal remnant. In Hebrews 11:32, several of these heroic judges whom God raised up during this dark period are listed for our inspiration.

> And what more shall I say? For time will fail me if I tell of Gideon, Barak, Samson, Jephthah, of David and Samuel and the prophets, who by faith conquered kingdoms, performed acts of righteousness, obtained promises, shut the mouths of lions. —Hebrews 11:32, 33

If you read Hebrews 11:33–40, you will be encouraged to see how God used ordinary individuals to perform extraordinary miracles. This means that if you consider yourself an ordinary believer, welcome to the club! God delights in all who humble themselves before Him, transforming ordinary lives so that He can use us all for His miraculous purposes.

One Man—Doing What Was Right in His Eyes

As we take a closer look at the life of Ruth, we will discover how the LORD used an ordinary Moabite woman to win her embittered mother-in-law back to faith in the God of Israel. Ruth also was the great-grandmother of King David.

The first verse of Ruth lets us know that the story begins at a time of famine.

> Now it came about in the days when the judges governed, that there was a famine in the land. And a certain man of Bethlehem in Judah went to sojourn in the land of Moab with his wife and his two sons. —Ruth 1:1

If there was a famine in your town, it would seem reasonable to temporarily move 40 miles away where bread is plentiful. The Hebrew word for "sojourn" (ger) indicates that as strangers they did not plan to live in Moab permanently, but return home after the famine had subsided. But why would Elimelech (whose name means "my God is King") move his family from his ancestral home of Bethlehem to the accursed nation of Moab? The Scriptures do not indicate that Elimelech sought the Lord's guidance in this decision, but that it seemed right in his own eyes to move there with his wife and two unmarried sons. The Scriptures teach repeatedly that if we seek God first, He will provide for all our needs. How ironic that Elimelech left Bethlehem—"House of Bread"—(*Beit Lechem* in Hebrew), in search of physical food in an accursed land. Had he sought the Lord and what God wanted to teach him through this famine, the outcome would surely have been different.

Seeking for Bread in My Famine

How do we respond during a season of famine? In my own spiritual journey, there have been times of physical scarcity and spiritual drought. Often, instead of seeking the Lord, I allowed worry to take over and I turn to alternative and unsatisfying sources for nourishment. Thankfully, over the years, I have been growing little by little into the same truths that

God desired to teach the children of Israel in the wilderness. God is clear about what He wants us to learn in times of famine.

> And He humbled you and let you be hungry, and fed you with manna which you did not know, nor did your fathers know, that He might make you understand that man does not live by bread alone, but man lives by everything that proceeds out of the mouth of the LORD." —Deuteronomy 8:3

Yeshua of Nazareth, at the very beginning of His earthly ministry, had been fasting and praying for 40 days. During this struggle, Yeshua repeats this verse from Deuteronomy to rebuke Satan.

> ...being tempted by the devil. And He (Yeshua) ate nothing during those days; and when they had ended, He became hungry. And the devil said to Him, "If You are the Son of God, tell this stone to become bread." And Yeshua answered him, "It is written, 'Man shall not live on bread alone.'" —Luke 4:2–4

Additionally, in the Sermon on the Mount, Yeshua gives His followers Divine teaching on the matter of food and our treasures (Matthew 6:24–32). This entire section gives us the ultimate cure for anxiety and worry. Yeshua provides us with His conclusion on all these matters.

> But seek first His kingdom and His righteousness; and all these things shall be added to you. Therefore do not be anxious for tomorrow; for tomorrow will care for itself. Each day has enough trouble of its own. —Matthew 6:33

King David also understood the absolute need to seek God first during times of famine.

> Better is the little of the righteous than the abundance of many wicked. For the arms of the wicked will be broken; But the LORD sustains the righteous. The LORD knows the days of the blameless; And their inheritance will be forever. They will not be ashamed in the time of evil; And in the days of famine they will have abundance. —Psalm 37:16–19

COMPASSION *and* REDEMPTION

David promises that in the days of famine, God's children will enjoy abundance and be satisfied. Yeshua taught us the same principle.

> Blessed are those who hunger and thirst for righteousness, for they shall be satisfied. —Matthew 5:6

In other words, if followers of Yeshua seek His Kingdom first, we will lack nothing; but, rather, we will always experience complete satisfaction—guaranteed!

David goes on to reiterate that when we follow the Lord, He will order and direct our spiritual walk in Him. There is beautiful assurance in Psalm 37, as David looks back over his life, declaring that God has never forsaken him or allowed his family to beg for bread.

> The steps of a man are established by the Lord; And He delights in his way. When he falls, he shall not be hurled headlong; Because the Lord is the One who holds his hand. I have been young, and now I am old; Yet I have not seen the righteous forsaken, Or his descendants begging bread. All day long he is gracious and lends; And his descendants are a blessing. —Psalm 37:23–26

Notice what David says in verse 24, that when he falls, God is still holding his hand. I find this so encouraging because I have fallen many times and despaired that God did not care about my situation or my need. During these times of famine, I would stumble in unbelief. Nevertheless, despite my unfaithfulness, I found God always faithful, never letting go of my hand. Even when I make mistakes, as soon as I turn back to God and confess to Him, He is always there to forgive and restore me to fellowship with Him. The same is true for you.

> If we confess our sins, He is faithful and righteous to forgive us our sins and to cleanse us from all unrighteousness. —1 John 1:9

Before we study Ruth's life, meditate on the Scriptures from this section.

RUTH

THOUGHTS AND REFLECTIONS:

1. Reflect on your own walk with the Lord. Are you giving Him first priority? Instead of being anxious about your problems do you seek Him, His Kingdom and His righteousness? Read Matthew 6 to reorient your priorities.

2. Consider the following definition of worry: "Worry is allowing problems and distress to come between you and the heart of God; it is the view that somehow God has lost control of the situation and you cannot trust Him. A legitimate concern presses us closer to the heart of God and causes us to lean and trust on Him all the more."
   [*Is that You Lord?* by Gary E Gilley in April 1, 2017]

   Ask yourself: Are my concerns drawing me closer to God or are my worries driving me away from Him? (Proverbs 12:25, Psalm 139:23–24)

3. Take time to praise the Lord for how He has brought you through the seasons of famines in your life. Thank Him for always holding your hand even when you fall. (Psalm 37:23–26)

4. Read Numbers 22–25 for the story of how the Moabites hired Balaam to curse Israel. Not only does this tale of the talking donkey read almost like a children's story, you will also discover that the details are more attention-grabbing than any fiction writer could imagine.

COMPASSION *and* REDEMPTION

8. WHERE DOES SHE GET SUCH COURAGE?

The end of Ruth 1:2b says, Now they entered the land of Moab and remained there. This indicates that Elimelech and his family were no longer just sojourners living as strangers in Moab. This statement is followed by very sad news.

> Then Elimelech, Naomi's husband, died; and she was left with her two sons. And they took for themselves Moabite women as wives; the name of the one was Orpah and the name of the other Ruth. And they lived there about ten years. —Ruth 1:3, 4

What was Naomi to do? They were already settled in Moab and even though her husband died, she does not return to Bethlehem but stays put and finds Moabite wives for her two sons. Despite their disobedience, God continued to oversee the situation and, in His providential power, was working all things together for good even as more unfortunate news follows. We learn in verse 5 that, after living in Moab for ten years, both of Naomi's sons die.

> Then Mahlon and Chilion, also died. So, [Naomi] was left without her children and her husband. —Ruth 1:5 (TLV)

Some of you can relate to Naomi's heartbreaking situation. Perhaps you have lost a husband and, years later, you still grieve and miss him every day. Can you imagine, on top of that grief, to lose your children as well? This immense heartbreak for Naomi is unbearable to even think about. For Naomi, this is not just about physical death but also the loss of her hopes and dreams which surely included sons and grandchildren who would carry on the family name. Where could Naomi find comfort for her situation? Where can any of us go when our dreams are shattered, and we find ourselves alone in tearful anguish?

Naomi needed to make a choice about her future. What should a daughter of the God of Israel do when faced with desperation and sorrow? The Scriptures reveal to us that Naomi had already turned away from her only source of true comfort, choosing instead to do what was right in her own eyes. She accused God of plotting harm against her. In her despair, Naomi forgot how the God of Israel had brought her ancestors out of Egypt and into the Promised Land.

RUTH

Before judging Naomi too harshly, I must ask, what do I do when I am overcome with grief and pain? Do I accuse the Lord of not caring and blame Him for any evil that befalls me? The Scriptures let us know that God's Word must be the resource for our lives at these critical times; that we can and must trust the Lord in every circumstance.

Ruth would also have been in mourning having just lost a husband and brother-in-law. Yet, she did not become bitter or estranged from God; rather, she became a woman of great determination and faith. As the story unfolds, we will see how God used Ruth to comfort Naomi and ultimately bring her back to the Lord.

News from Her Hometown—The House of Bread

Naomi's story continues:

> Then she arose with her daughters-in-law that she might return from the land of Moab, for she had heard in the land of Moab that the LORD had visited His people in giving them food. —Ruth 1:6

Naomi uses the Covenant name of God in this verse. Hearing that the famine was over and that Bethlehem, the house of Bread, was a viable option once more, Naomi decides to return home.

> And Naomi said to her two daughters-in-law, "Go, return each of you to her mother's house. May the LORD deal kindly with you as you have dealt with the dead and with me. May the LORD grant that you may find rest, each in the house of her husband." Then she kissed them, and they lifted up their voices and wept.—Ruth 1:8-9

> At first, however, they both protested: And they said to her, "No, but we will surely return with you to your people." —Ruth 1:10

One can almost hear the pent-up grief and anguish pouring out of Naomi as she explains, through her bitterness, that she is too old to have any more sons for them to marry. She then elaborates that; even if she could have more sons, it would not be practical for her daughters-in-law to wait until the sons were of marrying age. In verse 13, her cynicism and doubt about God's goodness is exposed as she continues to clarify the situation for them.

COMPASSION *and* REDEMPTION

Naomi questions her daughters-in-law and then slanders the Lord God of Israel:

> Would you therefore wait until they were grown? Would you therefore refrain from marrying? No, my daughters; for it is harder for me than for you, for the hand of the Lord has gone forth against me. —Ruth 1:13

With this explanation from her mother in law, Orpah is convinced, through tears, to return to her own people and to the gods of the Moabites. The addition of the phrase returning "to the gods of the Moabites" makes the break complete. The Moabites had many demonic gods with a chief demonic god named Chemosh, sometimes translated as "destroyer," or "fish god." These gods were opposed to the God of Israel.

With the departure of Orpah, Naomi makes one final attempt to dissuade Ruth from coming with her.

> And they lifted up their voices and wept again; and Orpah kissed her mother-in-law, but Ruth clung to her. Then she said, "Behold, your sister-in-law has gone back to her people and her gods; return after your sister-in-law." —Ruth 1:14, 15

Courage to Follow and to Care

To Naomi's surprise, Ruth refuses to return to her own people and their gods. It is evident that Ruth had already come to faith in the God of Israel as she states in her famous declaration to Naomi.

> But Ruth said, "Do not urge me to leave you or turn back from following you; for where you go, I will go, and where you lodge, I will lodge. Your people shall be my people, and your God, my God. "Where you die, I will die, and there I will be buried. Thus may the Lord do to me, and worse, if anything but death parts you and me." —Ruth 1:16

This testimony of faith is astounding. Her affirmation of the One True God confirms the theme that runs through the lives of these women in the genealogy of grace. Remember Tamar? Somehow through the weak witness of her father-in-law Judah, she sought the Lord and found Him to be her righteousness. Rahab, behind enemy walls, through hearing the accounts of God's miracles, sought the LORD and found His salvation. Now we see Ruth's heart and discover that she, too, became committed to the God of Israel. God's plan is unfolding for her after ten years of a childless marriage. And though Naomi wanted to leave her in Moab, Ruth chooses to follow Naomi, to live where she lives, to identify with her people and to follow her God. With no promises of security and no assurance of finding a husband or having children of her own, Ruth is "all in" with Naomi and Naomi's God. In spite of the bitter witness of her mother-in-law, Ruth completely gives herself to the God of Israel. Ruth's faith, commitment and strength are simply astonishing.

Ruth's determination was such that Naomi stopped arguing with her daughter-in-law.

> When she (Naomi) saw that she (Ruth) was determined to go with her, she said no more to her. —Ruth 1:18

The word for "determined" in Hebrew is *ametz*. It means to be resolute, courageous, and to strengthen. This same word is used in Deuteronomy 31:6–7 when Moses give his farewell address to the children of Israel. Moses exhorts Israel, "Be strong and courageous (*ametz*), do not be afraid or tremble at them, for the LORD your God is the one who goes with you. He will not fail you or forsake you." This command to "be strong and courageous" is also repeated 4 times in the first chapter of Joshua and again in Joshua 10:25. Each time this command is given, it confirms the strength and courage (*ametz*) God has promised to supply to both Joshua and the nation of Israel in the face of future challenges. Ruth found her courage and determination to follow Naomi from the LORD God of Israel. She had no guarantee of acceptance and provision; yet Ruth's heart was determined to follow after God.

When Naomi saw this courage (*ametz*) displayed by Ruth, she stopped trying to persuade Ruth to return to her people and their false gods. Where did Ruth receive such courage when she had no strength or courage of her own? Where, but from the Lord God of Israel. The LORD knew the plans He had for Ruth and Naomi. As Ruth sought the LORD with all her heart, she found Him. God directed her paths and continued to give her the courage she needed. Just as we discovered in the story of Tamar, the later writings in Jeremiah repeat a possible refrain from the life of Ruth.

COMPASSION *and* REDEMPTION

> "For I know the plans that I have for you," declares the LORD, "plans for welfare and not for calamity to give you a future and a hope." Then you will call upon Me and come and pray to Me, and I will listen to you. And you will seek Me and find Me, when you search for Me with all your heart." —Jeremiah 29:11–13

The same is true for us when we seek God. We can receive His resources including courage that He provides to accomplish His purposes in our lives. God does not want us to shrink back from living for Him. He continually gives us His strength and courage.

> For God has not given us a spirit of timidity, but of power and love and soundness of mind. —2 Timothy 1:7

IS THIS NAOMI?

The narrative continues; in verse 19 we learn that a noisy crowd gathers to receive Naomi and Ruth when they return to the House of Bread.

> And it came about when they had come to Bethlehem that all the city was stirred because of them, and the women said, "Is this Naomi?" —Ruth 1:19

Why were the women who knew Naomi in such disbelief? She may have had a few more grey hairs but, it was something else. Now, instead of the wealthy wife of Elimelech who left ten years earlier, Naomi appeared like a beggar.

> Naomi said to them, "Do not call me Naomi; call me *Mara*, for the Almighty has dealt very bitterly with me. I went out full, but the LORD has brought me back empty. Why do you call me Naomi, since the LORD has witnessed against me and the Almighty has afflicted me?" —Ruth 1: 20–21

The name Naomi is based on the Hebrew word for pleasant (*na'im*). One familiar place this word is used is in the psalms.

> Behold, how good and how pleasant (*na'im*) it is for brothers to dwell together in unity! —Psalm 133:1

By contrast, Naomi's loss of faith in God is clear as Naomi talks to the women of Bethlehem. For now, Naomi asks them to call her *Mara*—which means "bitter." This is remniscent of Passover when we eat *maror* (bitter herbs) to remind us of the bitterness of bondage. Naomi wants to remember her bitter life as she tells the women to call her *Mara*.

Notice also that Naomi tells them that the Almighty has dealt bitterly with her; and, furthermore, she accuses this same Almighty of testifying against her and afflicting her. Who is this Almighty One? In Hebrew the word "Almighty" is *Shaddai*, a word that describes a power that is all bountiful. Just like the word "mercy" is based on the mother's womb, this word *Shaddai* is from the root *shad*, the Hebrew word for a women's breast. *Shaddai* means one who pours out all blessings, both temporal and spiritual. Some of us may relate to the pouring out aspect of this word. I remember with my firstborn son, Joshua, I was eager to breastfeed but didn't have any idea what to expect. When my breasts became engorged with milk, there was so much milk that the pressure was painful. Without proper instruction as to how tiny Joshua should receive this nourishment, he could have choked on the abundance of milk. This is to emphasize that Almighty is not a stingy God who gives us a drop of mercy here and a drip of power there to use sparingly. On the contrary, the LORD refers to Himself throughout the Scriptures as *El Shaddai*, the Almighty God, the bountiful and all powerful One. The LORD God revealed Himself to Abram as *El Shaddai*.

> And when Abram was ninety years old and nine, the LORD appeared to Abram, and said unto him, I am the Almighty God; walk before me, and be thou perfect. —Genesis 17:1 (KJV)

Job's advice about the Almighty could have helped Naomi understand how to respond to the LORD.

> Behold, happy is the man whom God corrects: therefore, despise not thou the chastening of the Almighty. —Job 5:17

When Naomi accused the Almighty of afflicting her, she might have overlooked her family's own decision to leave Bethlehem. Even in her own words she tells the women that "I went out full," meaning when they left there was an abundance of food and supplies, but now she has returned "empty." In Naomi's mind, even though she left with plenty, she is now returning empty. What a false perception a bitter heart can give! Who was standing next to her? She completely disregarded Ruth, who had totally committed herself to her and was her constant encourager. Because of her bitterness toward the Lord, Naomi could not see Ruth, her most valuable blessing, standing right next to her.

There is good news as this narrative unfolds, for we see Naomi's life change as she discovers the abundant blessings God provides through Ruth's love and willingness to follow Naomi's instructions. The Lord draws Naomi back into the arms of El Shaddai. The Almighty God became Av HaRachamim, the Father of Mercies, to Naomi.

Surprised by Grace

In chapter two, Ruth takes center stage as the heroine of an unfolding love story. And, if there is a love story, there is also a hero.

> Now Naomi had a kinsman of her husband, a man of great wealth, of the family of Elimelech, whose name was Boaz.   —Ruth 2:1

We have already looked briefly at Boaz in our study of Rahab. Let's review Ruth 2:1 and see Boaz as the kinsman redeemer whom God used to restore Naomi and her family. In this verse Boaz is introduced as a very close relative of Naomi's husband. As we have already discussed, the Hebrew is chayil gibbor which literally means "a man of powerful might," and is sometimes translated "a man of great wealth."

In this short verse, a wealth of information is provided about our hero. Boaz is not only a very close relative to Naomi, he is also a man of valor and strength, with resources that could make a difference in the impoverished condition of Naomi and Ruth. Even his name, Boaz, means one who is "in strength."

Not Afraid of Back Breaking Work

Our love story picks up at the beginning of the barley harvest in early May—a perfect opportunity for Ruth to find work as a gleaner in the fields of Bethlehem.

To help the poor and the strangers, God commanded Israel not to reap the corners of their fields or gather the gleanings of the harvest. Gleaners were the poor and strangers who welcomed the opportunity to pick up the small pieces of grain that fell around the corners of the field so that they could have sustenance for themselves. (Leviticus 19:9–10) This was back-breaking work; but if the stranger was willing to bend over to find the grain that had fallen, there could be enough provision.

Bending low to gather the food from the ground reminds me of how the children of Israel were instructed to gather the manna in the wilderness. God supplied it in abundance every day; and on Friday, they gathered a double portion for the Sabbath. The point is that God could have had the manna hanging from trees. Oh wait, they were in the wilderness with very sparse vegetation; however, since nothing is impossible for God, He could have had baskets of *manna* appear daily at every door. Could it be that the Lord, even in the wilderness, was teaching His children how much He loves humility and the value of humbling themselves to gather their daily bread? Isaiah the prophet tells us where God delights to dwell.

> For thus says the high and exalted One Who lives forever, whose name is Holy, "I dwell on a high and holy place, and also with the contrite and lowly of spirit In order to revive the spirit of the lowly and to revive the heart of the contrite." —Isaiah 57:15

Ruth is not bothered by this menial work and even asks permission from Naomi to go glean in order that they might have food to eat. Let's take a closer look at how she phrases her request.

> And Ruth the Moabitess said to Naomi, "Please let me go to the field and glean among the ears of grain after one in whose sight I may find favor." And she said to her, "Go, my daughter." —Ruth 2:2

In Whose Sight I May Find Favor

This expression "in whose sight I may find favor" is used by a person of inferior status in reference to someone who is superior. One example of needing to find favor in God's sight is demonstrated in the life of Moses. His need for God's favor and grace is clearly seen in the conversation that Moses was having with God when it seemed after so much rebellion that the Lord would not continue to lead the children of Israel with His visible Presence. The *Complete Jewish Bible* version from Exodus 33:12–14 uses the expression "found favor in your sight" three times.

COMPASSION *and* REDEMPTION

> Moshe said to *ADONAI*, "Look, you say to me, 'Make these people move on!' But you haven't let me know whom you will be sending with me. Nevertheless, you have said, 'I know you by name,' and also, 'You have found favor in my sight.' Now, please, if it is really the case that I have found favor in your sight, show me your ways; so that I will understand you and continue finding favor in your sight. Moreover, keep on seeing this nation as your people." He answered, "Set your mind at rest. My Presence will go with you, after all." — Exodus 33:12–14 (CJB)

Like Moses, who knew he could not lead without God's favor and grace in his life, Ruth understood that as a stranger she would need to find grace or favor in the eyes of those who were harvesting the fields. Ruth's attitude shows Naomi that she is willing to work, but God will have to give her the open door of grace. Here we see the providential care at work in Ruth's life.

> So she departed and went and gleaned in the field after the reapers; and she happened to come to the portion of the field belonging to Boaz, who was of the family of Elimelech. —Ruth 2:3

Boaz, the owner of the field, appears and has a conversation with his head reaper:

> Then Boaz said to his servant who was in charge of the reapers, "Whose young woman is this?" And the servant in charge of the reapers answered and said, "She is the young Moabite woman who returned with Naomi from the land of Moab. And she said, 'Please let me glean and gather after the reapers among the sheaves.' Thus she came and has remained from the morning until now; she has been sitting in the house for a little while." —Ruth 2:5–7

Finding Favor in the Sight of Boaz

Boaz doesn't waste any time but immediately goes to Ruth.

> "Listen carefully, my daughter. Do not go to glean in another field; furthermore, do not go on from this one, but stay here with my maids. Let your eyes be on the field which they reap, and go after

RUTH

them. Indeed, I have commanded the servants not to touch you. When you are thirsty, go to the water jars and drink from what the servants draw." —Ruth 2:8–9

Boaz offers Ruth protection from those who would seek to do harm and prey upon the gleaners at the edges of the fields. Boaz puts Ruth among his women who are working in the fields so she will be safe and cared for while reaping. Ruth's answer reveals her humility and surprise at his gracious behavior.

Then she fell on her face, bowing to the ground and said to him, "Why have I found favor in your sight that you should take notice of me, since I am a foreigner?" —Ruth 2:10

What a blessed response Boaz gives to Ruth!

And Boaz answered and said to her, "All that you have done for your mother-in-law after the death of your husband has been fully reported to me, and how you left your father and your mother and the land of your birth, and came to a people that you did not previously know. "May the LORD reward your work, and your wages be full from the LORD, the God of Israel, under whose wings you have come to seek refuge." —Ruth 2:11

Now Ruth is no longer a stranger. Her faith in the God of Israel has brought her into the family of God. Boaz pronounces a blessing for her, asking God to reward her fully for all she has done, He asks that she would know His peace, His protection and His provision because she chose to find her safe haven in the God of Israel.

Is Ruth Getting Paid to Glean?

Let's take a closer look at Boaz's blessing of Ruth.

May the LORD reward your work, and your wages be full from the LORD, the God of Israel, under whose wings you have come to seek refuge." —Ruth 2:12

Do you think that Ruth was looking for a reward for her work? As a gleaner she was hoping to pick up enough pieces of grain to provide food for Naomi and herself. Her labor was a matter of survival in this new land.

So, what kind of a blessing was Boaz giving to Ruth? The word "reward" is based on the Hebrew word shalem, which indicates "completion." Shalem comes from the well-known Hebrew word Shalom which means peace, wholeness and completeness. Boaz was blessing Ruth as the Lord's daughter who would find wholeness in serving the God of Israel.

God wants the same blessing for us as His daughters. When we serve the Lord out of love, the reward we seek is to know that our labor is not in vain in the Lord, and that our ways are pleasing to Him. The imperfect tense of the verb shalem indicates that what God is presently doing through Ruth, He will continue to do in and through her life. Do you sometimes feel that your work for the Lord might be in vain? We are given His promise that everything we do for His glory will not be forgotten by God. On the contrary, our Heavenly Father is aware of our labors and wants us to understand that what we do for Him will reap eternal rewards. God desires for us to draw continually on His strength to accomplish His will. By relying on Him, our labor will bring Him the honor and glory He deserves. Paul's exhortations to the congregations at Colossi, Philippi, and Ephesus are for us as well.

> Whatever you do, do your work heartily, as for the Lord rather than for men; knowing that from the Lord you will receive the reward of the inheritance. It is the Lord Yeshua whom you serve.
> —Colossians 3:23

> Being confident of this, that he who began a good work in you will carry it on to completion until the day of Messiah Yeshua.
> —Philippians 1:6

> I can do everything through Him who gives me strength.
> —Philippians 4:13

> For by grace you have been saved through faith; and that not of yourselves, it is the gift of God; not as a result of works, that no one should boast. For we are His workmanship, created in Messiah Yeshua for good works, which God prepared beforehand, that we should walk in them.
> —Ephesians 2:8–10

RUTH

Ruth's Chosen Work

What were the works that God had prepared for Ruth? As she yielded herself to the God of Israel and was strengthened by Him, she became a blessing to not only her mother-in-law but to the whole house of Israel. Her job officially was "gleaner" but her work for the Lord was to be His instrument of blessing.

Depending on the various seasons of our lives, we all have had different jobs and varied roles. I received a new title when I became a first-time grandmother—a role I am loving! Many of you may have two or more full-time jobs that could include mother and another vocation such as teacher or attorney. Whatever season of life you are in, be encouraged by Paul to understand that you are serving the Messiah and that your labor is never in vain in the Lord.

> Therefore, my beloved brethren, be steadfast, immovable, always abounding in the work of the Lord, knowing that your toil is not in vain in the Lord. —1 Corinthians 15:58

The Lord is My Reward

Boaz pronounced a blessing over Ruth.

> May the LORD reward your work, and your wages be full from the LORD, the God of Israel, under whose wings you have come to seek refuge. —Ruth 2:12

We have taken a close look at the Hebrew word for reward (*shalem*) from the phrase, "May the LORD reward your work." In our study we saw that not only did the reward from the LORD recognize Ruth for her faithfulness to God, but this reward also acknowledged God's faithfulness to her.

The second phrase of Ruth 2:12, "and your wages be full from the LORD" features another Hebrew word that will encourage us. The Hebrew word for wages that Boaz uses here is maskoret, from the root *sacar*. This word for wages is first used when the Lord speaks to Abram in a vision:

> "Do not be afraid, Abram. I am your shield, your great reward." —Genesis 15:1 (NIV)

COMPASSION *and* REDEMPTION

The great reward (*sacar*) for Abram is the same reward for all who have the faith of Abraham. The reward is none other than God Himself!

Blaise Pascal, a famous French mathematician and philosopher, said, "There is a God-shaped vacuum in the heart of every man which cannot be filled by any created thing, but only by God the Creator, made known through Jesus Christ." In other words, it's only through Yeshua that our lives can be complete and fulfilled. He is our reward, the recompense that makes our life worth living. As the Messiah declares to His followers,

> The thief comes only to steal, and kill, and destroy; I came that they might have life, and might have it abundantly." —John 10:10

It's such a privilege to be given Yeshua's abundant, eternal life as my own. Oh, how He desires to bless us! We can have such hope each day because as Yeshua said to Paul,

> And He has said to me, "My grace is sufficient for you, for power is perfected in weakness." —2 Corinthians 12:9

> Now to him who is able to do immeasurably more than all we ask or imagine, according to his power that is at work within us.
> —Ephesians 3:20 (NIV)

The Ultimate Protection and Refuge

The conclusion of Boaz' blessing for Ruth is like the cherry on top of a delicious ice cream sundae.

> ...the God of Israel, under whose wings you have come to seek refuge." —Ruth 2:12b

The word refuge means to seek shelter, and implies having trust, confidence and dependence. Just like Ruth, whose hope in God was refuge, we can find this same shelter as we seek the Lord, acknowledging our need for His protection and security. We can praise God along with David.

> O taste and see that the LORD is good; How blessed is the man who takes refuge in Him! —Psalm 34:8

RUTH

The rest of the book of Ruth weaves together the beautiful love theme of Naomi's restoration from her bitterness to returning to belief in the goodness of God. Under Naomi's guidance, Ruth approaches Boaz at the end of the harvest requesting that he become her kinsman redeemer.

This Biblical concept of the kinsman redeemer is found in the book of Deuteronomy where the law of the levirate marriage is explained.

> When brothers live together and one of them dies and has no son, the wife of the deceased shall not be married outside the family to a strange man. Her husband's brother shall go in to her and take her to himself as wife and perform the duty of a husband's brother to her. And it shall be that the first-born whom she bears shall assume the name of his dead brother, that his name may not be blotted out from Israel. —Deuteronomy 25:5–6

Many commentators have traditionally understood the relationship of Ruth and Boaz to be part of a levirate marriage. (Josephus in *Antiquities of the Jews* 5:332–5)

Boaz is happy to redeem Ruth and the property of Naomi. But he had to ask another closer relative first, who, as it turns out, was unable to marry Ruth. This redemption transaction was a public affair, witnessed by all the elders and community of Bethlehem as recorded in chapter four.

> Then Boaz said to the elders and all the people, "You are witnesses today that I have bought from the hand of Naomi all that belonged to Elimelech and all that belonged to Chilion and Mahlon. "Moreover, I have acquired Ruth the Moabitess, the widow of Mahlon, to be my wife in order to raise up the name of the deceased on his inheritance, so that the name of the deceased may not be cut off from his brothers or from the court of his birth place; you are witnesses today." And all the people who were in the court, and the elders, said, "We are witnesses. May the LORD make the woman who is coming into your home like Rachel and Leah, both of whom built the house of Israel; and may you achieve wealth in Ephrathah and become famous in Bethlehem. "Moreover, may your house be like the house of Peretz whom Tamar bore to Judah, through the offspring which the LORD shall give you by this young woman."
> —Ruth 4:9–12

COMPASSION *and* REDEMPTION

Wow! What a blessing the elders give to Boaz—that his wife Ruth will build up the House of Israel. And in verse 12, our genealogy of grace is merged together with the house of Peretz the breaker. Are you getting the idea that this love story is full of blessing and surprising grace at every turn?

WEDDING BELLS AND A BABY BRING EVEN MORE BLESSINGS

> So Boaz took Ruth, and she became his wife, and he went in to her. And the LORD enabled her to conceive, and she gave birth to a son.
> —Ruth 4:13

It's important to note that it is the covenant God of Israel who makes it possible for Ruth to become pregnant and give birth. Remember how the women of Bethlehem responded to Naomi when she first arrived? They were incredulous as they looked on her poverty; however, the faith of just one Moabite woman and her willing kinsman redeemer changed everything! Now these same women add their own blessing to Naomi.

> Then the women said to Naomi, "Blessed is the LORD who has not left you without a redeemer today, and may his name become famous in Israel. May he also be to you a restorer of life and a sustainer of your old age; for your daughter-in-law, who loves you and is better to you than seven sons, has given birth to him." Then Naomi took the child and laid him in her lap, and became his nurse.   —Ruth 4:14–16

Talk about a turnaround! Naomi listens as these women proclaim that God has redeemed her—become her Goel, her Redeemer—through the provision of Boaz. The women also proclaim that this child will be "a restorer of life." In Hebrew, restore is *shuv*; and life is *nefesh*, which refers to the soul, the inner person that includes our desires. And don't miss verse 16 where we hear that Naomi is to be intimately involved in raising her grandson! It seems that these same women who bless Naomi also give Ruth's son his name.

> The women who were her neighbors gave it a name; they said, "A son has been born to Na'omi," and called it Oved. He was the father of Yishai the father of David.   —Ruth 4:17 (CJB)

RUTH

What a beautiful conclusion to this love story of redemption where God's grace is lavishly poured out to Ruth enabling her, in turn, to show God's mercy and lovingkindness to her mother-in-law. This two-fold love story exhibits much more than a simple romance and marriage. This love embraces the deep sacrificial relationship of Ruth toward her mother-in-law and the redeeming love of Boaz toward both Ruth and Naomi.

In the next section we will see how Oved, the son of Ruth and Boaz, points to Yeshua the Messiah of Israel as the Servant of the LORD.

Thoughts and Reflections

1. Consider how the Lord used Ruth to bring Naomi back to the God of Israel. Ask God to reveal someone who is struggling with bitterness and anger whom you can lovingly reach out to with the Good News of God's love and grace.

2. Take time to meditate on Ephesians 4:29–32 and Hebrews 12:11–15 asking the Lord to show you if there is bitterness in your heart that is grieving the Holy Spirit.

3. Think about the purpose of the work that you are doing considering these verses.

   Whatever you do, do your work heartily, as for the Lord rather than for men; knowing that from the Lord you will receive the reward of the inheritance. It is the Lord Messiah whom you serve.　　　　　—Colossians 3: 23-4

4. Read the book of Ruth (it's only four chapters!) at least four times. Ask the Lord to give you His insights into His Word so you can share with others the truth of His amazing grace.

COMPASSION *and* REDEMPTION

9. THE SERVANT OF THE LORD CAME FOR YOU

Let us review the sons thus far:

Tamar's son was Peretz, the breaker whose name was fulfilled in The Master of the Breakthrough as seen in the life of our Messiah.

Boaz was the second son we studied. His name meaning "in strength" was seen in his life of selfless redeeming love which pictured the Messiah Yeshua our Redeemer and our Strength.

The third son is Oved, and his name in Hebrew means servant. This name may not seem as exciting as "the breaker" and "one who is in strength" nevertheless my prayer is that we can understand the true meaning of being a servant and discover how Yeshua became the ultimate Servant to bring us His salvation.

We concluded the preceding chapter with the women of Bethlehem praying that Oved would be a "restorer of life" to Naomi. How could a helpless baby become a restorer of life? The book of Ruth is a microcosm of a universal problem to which we can all relate. Due to famine, death and unspeakable grief Naomi turns away from her God, yet she desperately needs to return to Him for the comfort He alone can provide. The word restore means to turn back, or turn from going your own way to following God's way.

Naomi had turned away from God and her hardened soul was full of sorrow and bitterness. But this was not the end of her story, which turned around as the book of Ruth unfolded. Instead of condemning Naomi, the God of Israel sent Ruth and Boaz to draw her back by His redeeming love. When the women of Bethlehem told Naomi that her grandson would be a restorer of life, they were prophesying about Oved's role as a servant. Naomi would need to seek the Lord as she cared for her grandson. That service would help restore her love for the Lord and give her reasons to praise God for working all things together for her good.

OVED—WHAT DOES IT REALLY MEAN TO BE A SERVANT?

One aspect of studying the Hebrew language that I love is discovering families of words from the same root and delving into their various usages and meanings. From one root comprised of usually three letters, families of words develop. *Oved* is a commonly used word throughout the Hebrew Scriptures. Both *Oved* and *Eved* are nouns for "servant" and carry the meaning of one who either works or worships. These words occur over 800 times in the Scriptures. The verb form *avad* occurs 289 times in

Scripture; and from this verb, we derive the noun *avodah*, which appears 145 times. Depending on the context the various forms of the word for "servant" can mean labor or worship. Below are just a few examples.

Here is one example of the noun *avodah* being used for "work."

> Man goes out to his work and to his labor (*avodah*) until evening."
> —Psalm 104:23

The verb form is used for "worship" when God gave Moses instructions as to what to say to Pharaoh.

> This is what the LORD says: Let my people go, so that they may worship (*avad*) me." —Exodus 8:1 (NIV)

The same verb appears again in King David's admonition:

> Serve (*avad*) the LORD with gladness; Come before Him with joyful singing. —Psalm 100:2

Isn't it interesting that this family of words convey both working in the fields as well as worshiping the God of Abraham, Isaac and Jacob. When God created mankind, His original desire for us was to have a life of worship and work fulfilled in our relationship with our Creator God. After sin entered the human equation, our work became hard labor and our worship of our Creator was completely broken. Only the Servant of the Lord could remedy this dilemma and bring us back to the true meaning of worship and work.

Oved's name points forward to the fact that we as believers are called not only to serve the LORD but one another as well. Most significantly this name of servant is ultimately fulfilled in Yeshua who came to fulfill His earthly ministry as the Servant of the LORD.

YESHUA IS EVED ADONAI—SERVANT OF THE LORD

Throughout His earthly ministry Yeshua taught His disciples the necessity of becoming a servant. As the time drew nearer when He would be sacrificed, Yeshua answered the mother of the sons of Zebedee regarding her request for her sons to have a place of prominence in Messiah's Kingdom.

COMPASSION *and* REDEMPTION

> Whoever wishes to become great among you shall be your servant, and whoever wishes to be first among you shall be your slave; just as the Son of Man did not come to be served, but to serve, and to give His life a ransom for many. —Matthew 20:26-28

In His teaching to this concerned mother, Yeshua explains that His primary reason for taking on human flesh is to serve and be the payment for our sins...to be the "restorer of life" for each of us. Paul recommends Messiah's humble service for our salvation as an example for us all.

> Have this attitude in yourselves which was also in Messiah Yeshua, who, although He existed in the form of God, did not regard equality with God a thing to be grasped, but emptied Himself, taking the form of a bond-servant, and being made in the likeness of men. And being found in appearance as a man, He humbled Himself by becoming obedient to the point of death, even death on a cross. —Philippians 2:5-8

A number of prophecies in the Hebrew Scriptures refer to Yeshua as the Servant of the LORD. To highlight one of these prophecies, let's go to Matthew chapter 12 where Yeshua is declaring to the Pharisees that because He is the Lord of the Shabbat, He has the authority to heal and do good on the Sabbath. Messiah heals the man with the withered hand and sets in motion the official rejection of Yeshua as the Pharisees counsel together to see how they could destroy Him. (Matthew 12: 8-14)

The next verses in Matthew explain that these things happened "in order that what was spoken through Isaiah the prophet might be fulfilled," Then Matthew quotes Isaiah 42.

> Behold, My Servant (*Eved*), whom I uphold; My chosen one in whom My soul delights. I have put My Spirit upon Him; He will bring forth justice to the nations. "He will not cry out or raise His voice, Nor make His voice heard in the street. "A bruised reed He will not break, And a dimly burning wick He will not extinguish; He will faithfully bring forth justice. "He will not be disheartened or crushed, until He has established justice in the earth; and the coastlands will wait expectantly for His law." Thus says God the LORD, Who created the heavens and stretched them out, Who spread out the earth and its offspring, Who

gives breath to the people on it, And spirit to those who walk in it, "I am the Lord, I have called you in righteousness, I will also hold you by the hand and watch over you, and I will appoint you as a covenant to the people, As a light to the nations, to open blind eyes, to bring out prisoners from the dungeon, and those who dwell in darkness from the prison. "I am the Lord, that is My name; I will not give My glory to another, nor My praise to graven images." —Isaiah 42:1–8

In this prophetic portion, God is speaking through Isaiah about His Chosen Servant and what He would do to bring justice for all and be a light to the nations. This theme is reiterated in Isaiah 49:6 where we are given additional aspects of what the Servant of the Lord would achieve. It was prophesied by Isaiah that only the Servant of the Lord could bring both Israel and the nations back to God. God speaks through the prophet in Isaiah 49:6 He says, "It is too small a thing that You should be My Servant To raise up the tribes of Jacob, and to restore the preserved ones of Israel; I will also make You a light of the nations so that My salvation may reach to the end of the earth."

When God proclaims: "so that My salvation may reach to the end of the earth," the phrase "my salvation" is Yeshuati in Hebrew. In other words, God's Yeshua is the Servant who will not only redeem Israel but will also bring salvation to all the nations of the world who come to Him.

A number of years ago, Sam and I were ministering in Bucharest, Romania at a Messianic Conference. In attendance was an Israeli who was antagonistic to the fact that Yeshua could be the Messiah. He challenged Sam with a question: "Can the name of Yeshua be found in our Hebrew Scriptures?" When Sam got together with him privately, he showed him Isaiah 49:6 where Yeshua is called *Yeshuati*—my Salvation. As this young Israeli man read these verses in Hebrew, the Lord opened his heart to consider Yeshua as his Savior. To God be the glory, by the end of the conference, he came to place his trust in Yeshua as his salvation.

In Isaiah 49:6, God also declares that His Servant will be a light to the nations. In the book of Ruth we have studied the example of Ruth, the Moabite and Boaz the Israelite who were brought together through their love for the God of Israel. A Gentile woman and a Jewish man are made one in Him by the grace of God. Paul testifies in Ephesians 2 that Messiah Yeshua brought salvation to Israel and to the nations. In Ephesians 2:12–22, Paul explains how Messiah became a servant to all of those who accepted His way of salvation. Only in Yeshua's shalom can both Jews and the nations be made one.

DO I REALLY NEED TO BE CALLED A SERVANT?
Is it possible to combine worship and work as we serve the Lord? In His letter to the congregation at Colossae, Paul writes for our instruction regarding being a servant of Yeshua.

> Whatever you do, do your work heartily, as for the Lord rather than for men; knowing that from the Lord you will receive the reward of the inheritance. It is the Lord Messiah whom you serve.
> —Colossians 3:23–24

What does being a servant mean for our lives as believers? As I was thinking about being Yeshua's servant, my summer jobs before my second year of college came to mind. At 19, I was a believer of three years, and I desired to put the Lord first in my life. Because of economic challenges I needed to earn money to return to college, so I decided to get two summer waitressing jobs. From 6am to 2pm, I worked at a coffee shop for the breakfast and lunch shifts; and then from 4–10pm, I worked at a diner for the dinner shift. To say I was exhausted would be an understatement. However, with my mother's support, keeping those uniforms clean and counting my tip money, I was able to keep this schedule going seven days a week for the entire summer.

If any of you have been a waitress (aka server), you know that it can be a challenge, not only to please the customers but to work with the restaurant owners. Each day I tried to read the Word and often took a small Bible to the dinner shift in case it was a slow evening. One night a group of eight men came in for dinner and noticed my Bible at my wait station and asked me about it. This gave me an opportunity to share how I was trying to follow the Lord and return to college to study for a teaching degree. It was a brief conversation, and they were my last customers of the evening. I should mention that this was not a high-end diner, but I was hoping for a decent tip in spite of their average bills. To my surprise, when I started cleaning the table under each of their plates were bills, ranging from $1 to $5. It seemed like $1000 each to me as I realized how much God loved me and was watching over me. The summer season was almost over, and the Lord certainly knew how weary I was. God understood my need to be encouraged because I was not sure if I would have enough funds to pay my fall tuition.

That evening God spoke to my heart and reinvigorated my faith to keep serving where I was and keep sharing the Lord with my bosses and other customers. I was reminded that I was serving the Lord and not cranky bosses or crabby customers. As much as I needed to make the money to pay my college tuition, I also knew what Messiah promised to "supply all my needs according to His riches in Messiah Yeshua." (Philippians 4:19) I did not want to worry about the funds because I also knew what Messiah taught in Luke 16:13 "No one can serve two masters. Either you will hate the one and love the other, or you will be devoted to the one and despise the other. You cannot serve both God and money." (NIV) These many years, later I continue to praise the Lord for allowing me the privilege to serve Him.

That classic Bob Dylan song "You Gotta Serve Somebody" reminds me that even though I may behave like I am the master of my own fate, I am always serving somebody. Dylan's lyrics go on to say, "It may be the devil or it may be the Lord, but you gotta serve somebody."

I want to serve the Lord with all my heart and soul and might. If we are indeed serving the ultimate Servant of the Lord then our lives will display the qualities of service Yeshua demonstrated in His earthly ministry. This service is possible because of His sacrificial love for us. We are empowered by the Holy Spirit to minister His redemption, compassion and new life to others as we continue to serve the King of kings.

Note: There are many fine commentaries that give verse-by-verse teaching on the book of Ruth. My favorite is *The Book of Ruth—Hope Fulfilled in the Redeemer's Grace* by my husband, Sam Nadler. (I'm a little biased!) In all seriousness, in his devotional commentary of Ruth, Sam gives wonderful exposition and extensive Jewish background, as well as great application for our lives. I highly recommend it!

For Thoughts and Reflections

1. Read Isaiah 52:13–15 and 53:11–12 prophecies written 700 years before Messiah came where God calls Yeshua "My Servant" in each section. Consider what these truths of His sacrifice mean for you. Take time to praise Yeshua, the Servant of the Lord.

COMPASSION *and* REDEMPTION

2. Isaiah 49 gives details about the role of *Eved Adonai*—Servant of the LORD. Read each portion and be encouraged. Here are a few:

   a. He brings freedom to those who are in bondage, and gives true love and hope to those who are discouraged. (49:8–13)

   b. The love that the Servant of the LORD gives is compared to the love of a compassionate mother for her child. (49:14–23)

   c. The chapter concludes with the hope of this Servant being compared to a victorious warrior. (49:24–26)

3. Consider the following questions about Yeshua the Servant of the LORD and what this means for you.

   a. Is Yeshua the Servant of the LORD, the restorer of your life? Have you accepted what He alone accomplished to bring you back into a relationship with God?

   b. As you follow in Yeshua's steps, this relationship should be growing. Your life should be maturing in worship, adoration and thanksgiving. Conclude by asking Him to use you as His servant. Yield your life to Him.

SECTION FOUR

בת שבע
BATHSHEBA

"and to David
was born Solomon
by her who had been
the wife of Uriah"
Matthew 1:6

10. No Stranger to the Palace

Matthew introduces the fourth woman in our genealogy of grace with the description of "her who had been the wife of Uriah."

Why would Matthew omit Bathsheba's name? Bathsheba was no longer Uriah's wife when she bore a son into the genealogy of Yeshua because, at that time, she was married to David, the King of Israel. Since our theme has been to demonstrate God's amazing grace as the thread that ties the lives of these women together, I believe that the mention of Uriah's name is another indication of God's grace. Even though Uriah was murdered at David's command, he was not forgotten in the inspired Scriptures.

The Hittites are mentioned throughout the Hebrew Scriptures as adversaries of the Israelites and the God of Israel. According to Genesis 10, they were the descendants of Heth, son of Canaan, who was the son of Ham, born of Noah (Genesis 10:1–6). Still, being a Hittite did not exclude him from being included in David's inner circle. (2 Samuel 23:39) Since he was serving David from the beginning of his reign, we can safely assume that Uriah had become a God-fearer who followed the God of Israel. Could including Uriah's name in the genealogy demonstrate how the LORD valued him, remembering him as an honorable person. Uriah's name is also mentioned in 1 Kings where the writer lauds David's greatness as King, except in the case of Uriah the Hittite.

> But for David's sake the LORD his God gave him a lamp in Jerusalem, to raise up his son after him and to establish Jerusalem; because David did what was right in the sight of the LORD and had not turned aside from anything that He commanded him all the days of his life, except in the case of Uriah the Hittite. —1 Kings 15:4-5

In the next section, we will examine murder, a sin despised by God, who considers every life precious. Although David was forgiven for his iniquities, God honors Uriah, David's murder victim, by recording his name in I Kings 15:4 and including him in the genealogy of Matthew.

Who is Bathsheba?

According to the Scriptures, Bathsheba was the daughter of an Israelite named Eliam (2 Samuel 11:3), one of the thirty-seven "mighty men of David." (2 Samuel 23:34) As a revered warrior, Eliam would likely have

BATHSHEBA

been a frequent guest at the palace. Even more impressive is the fact that Bathsheba's grandfather, Ahithophel was the chief counselor of David and ranked even above the priests, Abiathar and Jehoiada (1 Chronicles 27:33). So wise were Ahithophel's counsels that it was said of him, "it was as if a man had inquired at the oracle of God: so was all the counsel of Ahithophel both with David and with Absalom." (2 Samuel 16:23)

A Brief Historical Review and Setting

We have already met Tamar, Rahab and Ruth—all Gentiles from pagan cultures. Now we meet Bathsheba, an Israelite. As we have noted throughout this study, these Gentile women in the lineage of Messiah offer proof that the Jewish Messiah extended his blessings beyond Israel. Now, with the inclusion of this particular Jewish woman we will see that in Yeshua, the barrier between Jew and Gentile is broken down, and that the Jewish Messiah is also the Savior of all mankind.

When we began our historical account with Tamar, the children of Israel were comprised of a bunch of families. These families were then organized into 12 tribes who would wander in the wilderness for 40 years before entering the Promised Land. It was during that conquest that we met Rahab. In our study of Ruth, we learned that during the time of the Judges everyone in Israel was doing what was right in his own sight. And although God wanted to be their King, the Israelites demanded a human king so that they could be like all the other nations. After the period of the Judges, Israel chose a king to rule over them. King Saul was the people's choice, not God's choice. After Saul disobeyed the Lord, God chose David, a man after His own heart, to be their second king.

The Scriptures do not mention David's exact age when he was anointed by Samuel to become the next king of Israel, but it's generally agreed that he was in his late teens. We do know that David spent a number of years fleeing from Saul before he could enter Jerusalem and set up his throne. Again, there are differing opinions as to the exact amount of time, but many scholars agree that David was on the run from Saul for 10–13 years.

We do know that David was thirty years old when he became king, and that he reigned forty years. At Hebron he reigned over Judah seven years and six months, and in Jerusalem he reigned thirty-three years over all Israel and Judah. (2 Samuel 5:4-5)

COMPASSION *and* REDEMPTION

When we meet Bathsheba, the fourth woman in Matthew's genealogy, we are catapulted into the middle of King David's reign as King where the LORD is blessing David in the midst of his very successful rule.

THE KING STAYS HOME

The account of David's meeting with Bathsheba is intertwined with the background of Joab, the general of David's army. A military campaign was in progress and David sent Joab and the troops to lay siege to Rabbah, the key city of the Ammonites (2 Samuel 11:1, 16–17; 1 Chronicles 20:1–3). The Ammonite army had fled to the walled city of Rabbah; and Joab, along with the Israelite troops, were giving the Ammonites time to run out of food and water before they attacked. This army maneuvering would have taken place in the early spring as the winter rains were slowing down and the weather was growing warmer.

David would have been about 50 years of age. And though his advisors could have told him not to engage actively in warfare, David would have been expected to be with his troops on the field to develop strategy and offer moral leadership during the battles. Yet, for reasons known only to the king, while his troops went off to war, David decided to stay behind in Jerusalem. This is where history takes an unexpected and tragic turn.

THOUGHTS AND REFLECTIONS

1. Read 1 Samuel 16:1–13 when David was first chosen and anointed to be king over Israel by the prophet Samuel. According to verse 7, what was God looking for in Israel's next king? Consider some of the ways David showed his love and his heart for God during his reign?

2. In light of Yeshua's teaching to His disciples, consider your own life and the reason the LORD chose you to be His child. Take time to praise Him for His everlasting love and thank Him for how He has brought you to where you are now.

"This is My commandment, that you love one another, just as I have loved you. Greater love has no one than this, that one lay down his life for his friends. You are My friends, if you do what I command you. No longer do I call you slaves, for the slave does not know what his master is doing; but I have called you friends, for all things that I have heard from My Father I have made known to you. You did not choose Me, but I chose you, and appointed you, that you should go and bear fruit, and that your fruit should remain, that whatever you ask of the Father in My name, He may give to you. This I command you, that you love one another." —John 15:12–17

COMPASSION *and* REDEMPTION

11. FROM GRIEF TO GRACE

Bathsheba's story begins one night, while David is back at the palace in Jerusalem.

> Now when evening came David arose from his bed and walked around on the roof of the king's house, and from the roof he saw a woman bathing; and the woman was very beautiful in appearance. So David sent and inquired about the woman. And one said, "Is this not Bathsheba, the daughter of Eliam, the wife of Uriah the Hittite?" —2 Samuel 11:2

David had just gotten up out of his bed and was outside on his rooftop enjoying the refreshing early evening breezes as the sun was setting. Perhaps he was looking for that perfect sunset. While walking on his roof and taking in his magnificent view, he saw the form of a beautiful woman. When David asked about her, the reply came back to him, "Is this not Bathsheba, the daughter of Eliam, the wife of Uriah the Hittite?"

Wait a minute! Stop right here! When David heard Bathsheba's name and the name of her husband, Uriah, warning sirens should have started ringing in David's head. What happened to the man after God's own heart? David should have checked his lustful urges upon realizing that this was Bathsheba, a woman he had known since she was a small child. If he would have turned his heart toward heaven, the Lord could have brought to his mind her grandfather Ahitophel, who was one his most trusted advisors, her father, Eliam, a member of his elite guard, as well as her husband Uriah who had served him faithfully for many years. Alas, David's heart had turned away from the Lord and he was concerned solely with satisfying his own desires.

When I think about what must have been going through David's mind, I see it this way. David had already decided he'd rather stay home in his palace instead of fulfilling his duty to go to war. Even though his responsibility was to be with his soldiers providing encouragement and support, he is on his palace rooftop in the later afternoon. What follows is like a soap opera that we will title "As David's World Turns." If we could peek into David's rationale it might go something like this: "Hey I'm the King! I'm feeling energetic and vigorous after that nap. I'm also feeling bored and lonely. Poor me! If only there was something fun to do, someone to make me happy. Wait, who is that lovely lady I see in the distance?

BATHSHEBA

I can see her beautiful form and I want a closer look. In fact, I want to meet her. I'm the king, and I can do as I please. Surely she can give me some moments of happiness to spice up this monotonous day.

The Scriptures go on to tell us what David did.

> Then David sent messengers and took her when she came into him and he lay with her. (She had purified herself from her uncleanness). Then she returned to her house. The woman conceived and sent word to David, "I'm pregnant." —2 Samuel 11:4–5 (TLV)

Some commentators write that Bathsheba brought this on herself by being immodest and seductive. In my opinion, these ideas do a great disservice to Bathsheba. I believe that the most logical explanation is that Bathsheba was at the *mikveh*, the ritual purification bath for women seven days after the end of their monthly menstruation. She was bathing according to the requirements of the purity customs of her day. Therefore, she did not choose her bathing location or even the timing of it. The phrase "she had purified herself from her uncleanness" is in the past tense, indicating that when she went to the palace Bathsheba had already completed her menstrual period and was now ceremonially clean after visiting the *mikveh*.

David's palace rooftop would have been one of the highest buildings, if not the highest, in Jerusalem and from that height he saw her bathing. These ceremonial baths would have been situated in places where Jewish women could go monthly. A *mikveh* had to have a source of fresh running water, like an underground spring. It's doubtful that the walls of a *mikveh* would be tall enough to conceal Bathsheba from the prying eyes of David and his lofty, royal vantage point.

Bathsheba was not tempting, seducing, or manipulating David. On the contrary, she was engaging in a ceremonial act of ritual purification for holiness—bathing naked in the *mikveh* to cleanse herself from the uncleanness of menstruation.

Consider what this says about Bathsheba. It tells us that she was trying to be a follower of the God of Israel and to honor Him by obeying purity laws. No doubt, from a very young age as she grew up around the palace, she heard the accounts of God's miracles and faithfulness to His people. All her life she would have known only one earthly king of Israel who loved the God of Israel with all his heart. During those 20 years of David's rule, she would have seen David's heart for God. Do you think that she would have recited many of David's psalms as she worshipped the God of Israel? According to my research, Bathsheba was summoned by King David when she was only about 20 years old or even younger.

When David summoned her, it would have been an invitation she could not refuse. He was her king, the king of Israel, the most powerful man she had ever known, and probably twice her age.

Then, when Bathsheba was in David's presence, the word used to describe what David did to Bathsheba is that he took her. In Hebrew, took is *lakach*, which is a strong expression of force that can mean to take, get, fetch, lay hold of, seize, receive, acquire, bring, marry (take a wife), snatch and take away. (from the *Analytical Hebrew and Chaldee Lexicon*, Benjamin Davidson, Zondervan Publishing)

When David overpowered and seduced Bathsheba, he may have utilized his royal charm or even his physical strength. We can only surmise that she was overwhelmed, probably stunned, shocked, and terrified to displease him. She had probably idolized him her whole life. The Scriptures do not provide additional insight into Bathsheba's emotional disposition or state of mind. Her only words that are recorded in this entire scenario are found in the message she sent to David: "I am pregnant."

First Manipulation, Then Murder

This announcement of her pregnancy sets into motion King David's manipulation of the situation. David calls Uriah from the battlefield to visit Bathsheba so he would sleep with her in order to make it appear that the child in her womb was Uriah's rather than his own. Much to David's consternation this plan doesn't work. Uriah was a man of such integrity and an honorable soldier that he did not want to have "pleasure with his wife" while his men were fighting the battles of David's kingdom.

When this plan fails, David plots murder to eliminate Uriah. He orders Joab to make Uriah's death inevitable on the battlefield. After the announcement that Uriah had been killed David gives Bathsheba time to mourn her husband, then takes her as his wife.

The Scriptures are crystal clear regarding the LORD's response.

> Now, when the wife of Uriah heard that Uriah, her husband, was dead, she mourned for her husband. When the time of mourning was over, David sent and brought her to his house and she became

BATHSHEBA

his wife; then she bore him a son. But the thing that David had done was evil in the sight of the LORD. —2 Samuel 11:26–27

It is difficult to consider what David must have been thinking when he plotted Uriah's death and claimed Bathsheba as his own, making the palace of the king of Israel a place of intrigue, polluted with his sordid schemes and secrets.

God's Mercy through Nathan

God sends the prophet Nathan to confront David regarding this evil that he had committed. He had sinned not only in the sight of Bathsheba and those in his kingdom; but, more importantly, David sinned in the sight of Almighty God.

We continually need God's wisdom to help us communicate with our friends, family members and those in our congregations. Nathan, the prophet, also needed great wisdom from God to speak to a disobedient king. What a difficult task, to confront David who had been living in lies and denial for many months. Instead of barging in with a "repent or perish" message, with God's guidance, Nathan tells David a story of two men who lived in the same city. One of these men was very, very rich; and the other was very, very poor. The rich man owned abundant flocks in contrast to the poor man who had one baby lamb. This baby lamb was beloved by his family so much so that his children would feed this lamb at the dinner table and even have this lamb sleep in their beds with them. Many of you animal lovers are relating to this poor man as your cute puppies and your snuggly kittens eat from your tables, sleep in your beds and are beloved members of the family. Nathan explains to David that this little ewe lamb was like a daughter to the poor man. Nathan understood that any interesting story needs a problem to resolve. The conflict arises when a traveler comes to the city and visits the rich man. Hospitality demands that the rich man provide the traveler with a good meal; however, this wealthy man did not want to spare any lambs from his well-stocked flocks. Nathan describes what happened next.

> "Now a traveler came to the rich man, and he was unwilling to take from his own flock or his own herd to prepare for the wayfarer who had come to him; rather he took the poor man's ewe lamb and prepared it for the man who had come to him." —2 Samuel 12:4

COMPASSION *and* REDEMPTION

It is intriguing that in this verse the same Hebrew word that was used to describe how David took Bathsheba is used twice. The rich man was unwilling to take (*lakach*) his own lamb but rather took (*lakach*) the poor man's little ewe lamb.

David's response to Nathan's dramatic story is immediate and full of indignation.

> Then David's anger burned greatly against the man, and he said to Nathan, As the LORD lives, surely the man who has done this deserves to die. "And he must make restitution for the lamb fourfold, because he did this thing and had no compassion."
> —2 Samuel 12:5–6

In spite of David's rage, Nathan confronts him with God's message of coming judgment on him, his household and his kingdom. After Nathan declares, "You are the man!" he provides a list to remind David that the LORD was the One who anointed him and gave him all he had. Nathan then adds a phrase that strikes my heart in verse 8, "If that had been too little, I would have added to you many more things like these!" David had forgotten that the God he served was a God of abundant blessings and lovingkindness, a God who would not withhold any good thing from his beloved David.

"I Have Sinned Against the Lord"

After hearing these stern rebukes and consequential judgments from God, David's rage turns to repentance. He acknowledges his sin to Nathan and to God. Then David said to Nathan,

> I have sinned against the LORD. —2 Samuel 12:13a

David appeals to God's lovingkindness and His great compassion. It was at this time, after his adultery with Bathsheba, his murder of Uriah, and being confronted by Nathan the prophet that David wrote his confession to God in Psalm 51.

> For the director of music. A psalm of David. When the prophet Nathan came to him after David had committed adultery with Bathsheba. Have mercy on me, O God, according to your unfailing

love; according to your great compassion blot out my transgressions. Wash away all my iniquity and cleanse me from my sin. For I know my transgressions, and my sin is always before me. Against you, you only, have I sinned and done what is evil in your sight; so you are right in your verdict and justified when you judge.
—Psalm 51:1–4 (NIV)

David understood that although he had hurt Bathsheba and many others along the way, the Lord was his ultimate judge and he needed God's forgiveness first and foremost. David also makes a promise to the Lord within His prayer of contrition in Psalm 51:10–13. In verse 13 David assures God that he will teach other sinners about the joy of forgiveness with the goal of many turning back to worship God.

Create in me a pure heart, O God, and renew a steadfast spirit within me. Do not cast me from your presence or take your Holy Spirit from me. Restore to me the joy of your salvation and grant me a willing spirit, to sustain me. Then I will teach transgressors your ways, so that sinners will turn back to you.
—Psalm 51:10 (NIV)

David's promise in Psalm 51 can be found in Psalm 32, which many scholars believe David wrote just after his Psalm 51 confession. In the section "What Can Psalm 32 Mean for Your Life?" we will explore this psalm verse by verse to learn what God can teach us about His forgiveness through the pen of David. This said, in Psalm 32:3–4 we catch a glimpse as to what is was like for Bathsheba to be in the palace with David during those months when David was estranged from the LORD.

When I kept silent about my sin, my body wasted away through my groaning all day long. For day and night Your hand was heavy upon me; my vitality was drained away as with the fever heat of summer. Selah.
—Psalm 32:3

Bathsheba would have had the joy of being pregnant and expecting her first child but according to these verses the atmosphere around the palace bedroom and throne room was oppressive, with all of David's moaning, groaning, and sickness caused by his disobedience.

COMPASSION *and* REDEMPTION

It's easy to point a finger at David because he messed up so royally. However, we need to ask ourselves, have we grieved God's heart by sinning against him? I can certainly answer yes as I identify with King David in his pride: telling lies and even covering up his lies to stir up strife. Furthermore, when I do not confess my sins I know I am grieving the Holy Spirit of God who dwells in me. The result of quenching the Holy Spirit also quenches my vitality and commitment to live for the Lord. I am miserable and have no desire to be God's earthen vessel of grace and bless the lives of others.

Forgiveness, Consequences, and a Turning Point

Encouraged by David's repentance, Nathan delivers another message from the Lord to David.

> Nathan said to David, "The LORD also has taken away your sin; you shall not die. "However, because by this deed you have given occasion to the enemies of the LORD to blaspheme, the child also that is born to you shall surely die." —2 Samuel 12:13b-14

What wonderful news! David is forgiven and will live, even though according to the Law of Moses, his sins are punishable by death; however, this good news is coupled with sad news, especially for Bathsheba. Their newborn son would die. Why? The Scriptures in verse 14 are precise to let us know that it's because of what David did. His sins gave opportunity for God's enemies to despise and curse the LORD's Holy Name.

It seems so harsh, especially to a mother's ears, that such a pronouncement of death would come to their innocent infant who had done nothing wrong. I am reminded that the Lord's ways are not my ways and His thoughts are higher than mine for the Lord uses this sorrowful situation to teach us all a truth about what happens when small children die. David gives us this promise as he answers the elders and servants of his household about the death of his son.

> And David said, "While the child was still alive, I fasted and wept; for I said, 'Who knows, the LORD may be gracious to me, that the child may live.' But now he has died; why should I fast? Can I bring him back again? I shall go to him, but he will not return to me." —2 Samuel 12:22-23

BATHSHEBA

This encouraging reality echoes throughout history and continues to comfort the hearts of millions of parents with the fact that we will one day see our children who have gone on before us. I think of my third baby that I miscarried and never knew. I truly believe that I will be rejoined with this child that I carried in my womb for such a short time; and that, one day, we will rejoice in heaven together before the KING OF KINGS.

David must have had this same comfort from God because the next thing he does is truly remarkable. This is the first time we read of David reaching out to Bathsheba with comfort and love.

> Then David comforted his wife Bathsheba, and went in to her and lay with her; and she gave birth to a son, and he named him Solomon (peaceful/man of peace). Now the LORD loved him and sent word through Nathan, the prophet, and he named him *Yedidiah* (Beloved of the LORD) for the LORD's sake. —2 Samuel 12:24–25

How was David able to become a comforting husband instead of a lustful king who just wanted to possess Bathsheba's body? If we read what David wrote in both Psalm 51 and Psalm 32, we gain insight into his frame of mind before he confessed his sins and after he confessed his sins. We can understand like King David, that the Lord is a God of new beginnings for He alone can create a new heart in us as we confess our sins and seek His forgiveness. If God can forgive and restore King David and Bathsheba, will He do any less for you?

We must pay attention to what David is saying to us from his life that was restored to God. He is speaking from experience, teaching us how we can discover God's ways for happiness and blessing of forgiveness. First, let's consider why so few of us experience the joy of our salvation even as His daughters. Perhaps in your past you sinned in such a way that you feel God can never really forgive you or, more accurately, you can never really forgive yourself. You may be living under a cloud of self-condemnation and find it difficult to accept God's forgiveness and redeeming love for you. Let's learn together from the life of David.

David had completely blown it, destroying his reputation and impugning God's character in the process. It may be difficult for us to understand how damaging David's sins were. To put this in perspective I want to suggest to you God's top list of sins that He hates and compare the sins that David had committed.

COMPASSION *and* REDEMPTION

> There are six things which the LORD hates, Yes, seven which are an abomination to Him: Haughty eyes, a lying tongue, and hands that shed innocent blood, a heart that devises wicked plans, Feet that run rapidly to evil, a false witness who utters lies, and one who spreads strife among brothers. —Proverbs 6:16–19

David had haughty eyes—a synonym for pride. In 2 Samuel 11:1–4 David displayed his pride and egotism by deciding not to remain with his soldiers. Instead of submitting to God and doing his job as king, he stayed behind and shirked his responsibility. He used his position of power to seduce and overpower Bathsheba, to gratify is lustful desires and inflated ego. This is similar to the fall of Satan as it is described in Isaiah 14:12–14. Satan had the position of chief worship leader in heaven; but, in his arrogance and pride, he desired to ascend above the throne of God. When David carried out his prideful actions, he was emulating the actions of the evil one.

The next sin that God hates is a lying tongue. David was caught up in a quagmire of lies. He lied to Bathsheba, to Uriah and to many in the palace. Again, David was following Satan.

> "You are of your father the devil, and you want to do the desires of your father. He was a murderer from the beginning, and does not stand in the truth, because there is no truth in him. Whenever he speaks a lie, he speaks from his own nature; for he is a liar, and the father of lies."
> —John 8:44a

The third sin God hates is described with the phrase "hands that shed innocent blood." David deliberately had Uriah murdered. I believe in a court of law this would be regarded as a premeditated crime. Here, once more, David is following in the footsteps of Satan who was a "murderer from the beginning." (John 8:44)

"A heart that plots to do evil schemes" is the fourth sin listed. David used his military and executive skills to cook up sinister ways to cover his sins. In Ephesians, we are warned that it is Satan who schemes to thwart the plan of God; and for this reason we are instructed to:

> Put on the full armor of God, that you may be able to stand firm against the schemes of the devil." —Ephesians 6:11

BATHSHEBA

The fifth sin listed is "feet that run quickly to do evil." Instead of confessing his selfish schemes and turning back to God, David ran away from God and continued to run headlong down an evil path as he kept silent about his deceitful deeds for almost a year.

The last two sins are listed as being a false witness and stirring up discord between brothers. Can you imagine the lying and strife that was happening in the palace while David remained silent about his sins?

We can see at a glance that David had grievously offended the LORD. Nevertheless, as much as David sinned against Him, the LORD cared enough about his servant to have Nathan, the prophet, confront him. When David acknowledged his sins, the Lord forgave him completely enabling him to be a source of comfort to Bathsheba and to continue to rule over Israel for another 20 years.

WHAT CAN PSALM 32 MEAN FOR YOUR LIFE?

David gives us the top two reasons that should give us cause to be happy in the midst of this evil generation.

> Blessed is the one whose transgressions are forgiven, whose sins are covered. Blessed is the one whose sin the LORD does not count against them and in whose spirit, is no deceit. —Psalm 32:1, 2 (NIV)

This word "blessed" can also be translated happy, and it speaks of the total forgiveness that we find in the Lord. As we accept God's provision for and acceptance of us, we will grow in our understanding of how to find happiness by God's design. This teaching that poured out of David's contrite heart under the influence of the Holy Spirit would become a comfort to Bathsheba, as well. These eternal truths would restore Bathsheba and heal her grieving heart as she realized that she, too, was accepted and forgiven by her God. Instead of growing bitter and cynical, she would be filled with God's lovingkindness and courage to raise her son Solomon and continue to be affirming to David. Remember, if God can forgive and restore King David and Bathsheba, will He do any less for you?

In traditional Judaism, Psalm 32 is read every year at the close of Yom Kippur—the Day of Atonement. When the Temple still stood in Jerusalem, the Day of Atonement was the one time each year when the High Priest of Israel entered the Holy of Holies to seek atonement on behalf of the congregation of Israel. An important tradition that was observed each year at that time concerned two goats. The High Priest would cast lots over the two goats: one would be set aside for the LORD as a sin offering, and the other would become the scapegoat. Each of these goats represented the provision of God's forgiveness. Total payment for iniquities was represented in the sin offering and total removal of these sins was pictured as the High Priest confessed the nation's sins and transferred them onto the scapegoat to make atonement for the nation. The scapegoat was then driven into the wilderness to a high, rocky precipice in the Judean desert never to be seen again. As it disappeared it carried away the sins of the people. (Leviticus 16:7–10)

This concept of having our sins removed and never brought up again is found in David's words.

> How happy is the one whose transgression is forgiven, whose sin is covered. —Psalm 32:1

God cannot permit sin in His presence. However, through Messiah, we are accepted because we are forgiven, and our sins are covered. In Hebrew "forgiven" means the removal of a burden. This concept of removal of the burden of sin is foreshadowed by the scapegoat of Yom Kippur. Just as the scapegoat is chosen to carry the sins of the people into the wilderness, never to be seen again; so also, because of Yeshua's sacrifice, our sins are forever hidden from God's sight. In other words, when God covers our sins they are permanently removed.

The prophet Micah says our sins are cast into the depths of the sea.

> Who is a God like You, who pardons iniquity and passes over the rebellious act of the remnant of His possession? He does not retain His anger forever, because He delights in unchanging love. He will again have compassion on us; He will tread our iniquities under foot. Yes, You will cast (*tashlich*) all their sins into the depths of the sea. —Micah 7:18, 19

We also see this idea of permanent removal of our sins from David in another psalm.

> For as high as the heavens are above the earth, So great is His lovingkindness toward those who fear Him. As far as the east is

from the west, So far has He removed our transgressions from us. Just as a father has compassion on his children, So the LORD has compassion on those who fear Him. —Psalm 103:11–13

Yeshua fulfilled this picture of the scapegoat removing sin by taking away our sins permanently, even as John the Baptizer declared. The next day John saw Yeshua coming to him, and said, "Behold, the Lamb of God who takes away the sin of the world! (John 1:29) Yeshua also fulfills this cleansing power every time we agree with God about our sins and confess them to Him.

If we confess our sins, He is faithful and righteous to forgive us our sins and to cleanse us from all unrighteousness. —1 John 1:9

Wait, that's not all! We have another reason given as to why we who are forgiven should be happy and feel blessed.

How blessed (happy) is the person to whom the LORD does not impute iniquity, and in whose spirit, there is no deceit! —Psalm 32:2

Have you ever been in a drive-thru lane, like at Chick-Fil-A, and when you tried to pay for your food, the server told you, "Your bill has already been covered by the person in front of you. Have a great day!" How did you feel when you found out your bill was paid in full?

The word "impute" means "charge to one's account," and in Yeshua, all debts are cancelled because your sins were charged to Him on the cross. Your sin bill is stamped "PAID IN FULL" by the blood of Yeshua. In order to live in light of what God has already done, it is essential for us to understand that our sins are forever removed.

TOTALLY ACCEPTED

What does it mean to be accepted? Some synonyms include to be acknowledged, recognized, approved and supported. The anonyms of acceptance are rejection, exclusion, abandonment, disapproval and unsupported.

Why do we check our Facebook page 50 times a day? Why do we wish to be in the most popular group whether at school, at work, or even in the congregation? We long to be accepted? Well, here is the most extraordinary news flash and spiritual truth for today. Because of what Yeshua has done for you by removing your sins, God accepts you completely. You are clothed in Messiah's perfect righteousness and wrapped in His garments of salvation that don't wash off in the shower. This truth is affirmed throughout Scripture.

> I delight greatly in the LORD; my soul rejoices in my God. For he has clothed me with garments of salvation and arrayed me in a robe of his righteousness, as a bridegroom adorns his head like a priest, and as a bride adorns herself with her jewels. —Isaiah 61:10 (NIV)

God's acceptance of us has nothing to do with our own works. The Apostle Paul wrote this to the Corinthian congregation and to us as well.

> (The Father) made Him (Yeshua) who knew no sin to be sin on our behalf, that we might become the righteousness of God in Him. —2 Corinthians 5:21

Can we agree that this acceptance by God, standing before Him in the righteous robes given to us by Yeshua, can be our starting point each morning? Every morning, I desire to be thankful and acknowledge who I am in Messiah! Every day, I can begin anew by recognizing my identity in Him.

SELAH—STOP AND THINK ABOUT IT!
How can we live in the "no condemnation zone" and experience the fullness of God's joy in our lives?
We can begin with this instruction for a guilt free life:

> When I kept silent about my sin, my body wasted away through my groaning all day long. For day and night Your hand was heavy upon me; my vitality was drained away as with the fever heat of summer. Selah. I acknowledged my sin to You, and my iniquity I did not hide; I said, "I will confess my transgressions to the LORD"; and You did forgive the guilt of my sin. *Selah.* —Psalm 32:3–5

The Hebrew word *selah* is found only in the poetic books of the Hebrew Scriptures. It occurs 71 times in the Psalms and three times in

Habakkuk. The exact meaning is unknown, but many scholars consider it a musical term that means to pause or reflect. A signal to stop and think about what the writer is saying, because it is vitally important. When we see the word *selah* we should pause and carefully weigh what we have just read or heard, opening our hearts in praise to God.

> All the earth bows down to you; they sing praise to you, they sing the praises of your name. *Selah*! —Psalm 66:4 (CJB)

Note that in Psalm 32 above, David uses the word *selah* after verses 4 and 5 as he first gives the condition of not confessing his sins and then the consequences of both acknowledging his sins and confessing his sins to the Lord. The first word "acknowledge" in the Hebrew is a word we discussed in the Tamar section and also in our discussion of Boaz: *yadah* means to know or be aware. In other words, when David admitted his sin to the LORD, he acknowledged all the rotten stuff he had done. In Psalm 32:5 notice the phrase "my iniquity I did not hide," tells us that David did not try to whitewash any of his wretched attitudes and actions.

David goes on to say that he will confess his transgressions to the Lord. This word "confess" describes casting all his sins on the Lord and the result is God removing the guilt of that sin. Just as David says:

> I will confess my transgressions to the LORD; and You did forgive the guilt of my sin. *Selah*. —Psalm 32:5b

Remember, according to Romans 8:1, There is therefore now no condemnation for those who are in Messiah Yeshua. Do you feel guilty about something? Do not live in condemnation but rather cast your cares and your burden of guilt upon God, accept His forgiveness and walk in His freedom. You are accepted as the beloved of the Most High God.

Psalm 32 contains a beautiful promise to us who are His children. We are promised that when the troubles come like a great flood of waters, His protection will be there for us, surrounding us as we trust and hide in Him. As you read these verses, let them reaffirm God's care for you and His assurance to surround you with His songs of deliverance.

> Therefore, let everyone who is godly pray to You in a time when You may be found; Surely in a flood of great waters they shall not reach

COMPASSION *and* REDEMPTION

him. You are my hiding place; You preserve me from trouble; You surround me with songs of deliverance. *Selah.* —Psalm 32:6–7

At the end of this section, another Selah tells us to pause and reflect upon how the LORD is our place of refuge. He will preserve and guard us; He will protect us during trouble.

Psalm 32 also promises that God will teach us and show us His path for our lives. However, God also warns us not to be like a horse or mule who have no understanding but need the restraints of the bit and bridle to guide them.

> I will instruct you and teach you in the way which you should go; I will counsel you with My eye upon you. Do not be as the horse or as the mule, which have no understanding, whose trappings include bit and bridle to hold them in check, otherwise they will not come near to you. Many are the sorrows of the wicked; but he who trusts in the LORD, lovingkindness shall surround him. —Psalm 32:8–10

What can this say to us? When we submit to God's authority and guidance, we may not require those restraints, like a stubborn horse. When we put our confidence in the LORD, His lovingkindness will surround us.

The final verse of this Psalm reiterates the fact that in our blessedness or being happy, we have reason to be glad, to rejoice and shout for joy. We can end this section with the good news of forgiveness and acceptance found in Psalm 32. We can affirm along with Bathsheba and David,

> Be glad in the LORD and rejoice, you righteous ones, And shout for joy, all you who are upright in heart. —Psalm 32:11

THOUGHTS AND REFLECTIONS

1. Consider what David did that caused others to blaspheme the Holy One of Israel. How did his behavior grieve God's heart? Compare David's sins with the seven sins that God hates in Proverbs 6:16.

    Take time to reevaluate your own life and ask the LORD to reveal any secret sins. As you consider how you may have sinned against the Lord, take time to confess and accept His total forgiveness. Meditate on Psalm 32 and praise the Lord for His complete forgiveness in Messiah Yeshua and your acceptance into His family.

2. Affirm these truths and think of more truths that are based on God's promises to you:

   I am totally forgiven of all my sins and accepted as His daughter and called His Beloved. —1 John 1:1–3

   I am clothed in the righteousness of Yeshua's salvation and am counted as righteous. —Isaiah 61:10

   I do not have to carry the guilt of any of my sins because God has forgiven me and removed them forever.
   —Romans 8:1

COMPASSION *and* REDEMPTION

12. A Greater Than Solomon is Here

We ended our last section discussing how David was able to bring comfort to Bathsheba through his renewed faith. Psalm 32 might have been a message especially for her as well as for us today. It explains that no matter the gravity of the sins we commit, we can live in light of the Lord's acceptance and forgiveness.

Before we study the life of Solomon, David and Bathsheba's second son, recall that the first son of David and Bathsheba died at just seven days old. The Scriptures do not give us his name because he died before his circumcision on the eighth day when he would have been named. Even though we don't have his name recorded in the Scriptures, I believe that the LORD who formed this first child in Bathsheba's womb knows his name and this child is rejoicing in heaven today.

The birth of Solomon, their second son, is quite a contrast to the first son who died. He is given two names at his birth. David calls his baby Solomon (Shlomo) which means "man of peace" and Nathan the prophet names him Yedidiah which means "beloved of God."

> Now the LORD loved him and sent word through Nathan, the prophet, and he named him Yedidiah for the LORD's sake."
> —2 Samuel 12:24b, 25

What a wonderful God we serve who reminded David and Bathsheba of His love for their son through the name Yedidiah.

God's Answer to Solomon's Request

Of all the sons we have studied thus far, Solomon is referenced most in the Scriptures. A prolific writer himself, he penned several books in the Hebrew Scriptures including Proverbs, Ecclesiastes, The Song of Solomon and Psalm 72 and Psalm 127.

King Solomon was renowned for his God-given wisdom.

In Gibeon the LORD appeared to Solomon in a dream at night; and God said, "Ask what you wish me to give you." Solomon asked the Lord for an understanding heart to know how to judge the people and have God's discernment in his decisions. The Lord was pleased to not only answer Solomon's request but also bestow on Solomon unlimited riches and honor. (I Kings 3:5–15)

Solomon's wisdom, wealth and writing all flowed from the blessings and provisions of God. He gave Solomon everything he needed to be a wise king. His crowning achievement was the building of the Holy Temple in Jerusalem. In I Kings 10:23–24, we have a brief synopsis of his ongoing reign.

Even though it was the desire of his father David's heart to build a Temple for the Lord, God gave David the assurance that Solomon would be the one to build the temple. In 1 Chronicles 22:5 David says that his son, Solomon, although young and inexperienced, would build the Lord "an exceedingly magnificent" temple that would be "famous and glorious throughout all the lands." Before his death, David made sure that Solomon had ample preparations in place to build this temple for the Lord.

Solomon's Esteem for His Mother

The Scriptures do not offer many details about Solomon's relationship with his mother; however, we can learn much from a public exchange they had when Solomon became king of Israel. Shortly after Solomon ascended the throne and after the death of David we have a glimpse of the respect that Solomon gave to his mother.

> So, Bathsheba went to King Solomon to speak to him for Adonijah. And the king arose to meet her, bowed before her, and sat on his throne; then he had a throne set for the king's mother, and she sat on his right. —I Kings 2:19

Notice how Solomon greets his mother and honors her before the entire court. He humbles himself as he bows before her. He has a throne for her installed on his right side—the place of honor, possibly equal honor to the king himself. This was the degree to which he respected his mother Bathsheba.

Who is Lemuel and who is his mother?

Proverbs 31 was written by King Lemuel who was taught by his mother. Lemuel means "toward God" or "devoted to God," but there is no information about this king. Some commentators think that Lemuel is another name for Solomon, which would mean that this teaching was given to him by his mother Bathsheba.

I found the following information to be helpful as I struggled to understand how this portion relates to Solomon and Bathsheba:

COMPASSION *and* REDEMPTION

One wonders in concert with Jewish tradition if King Lemuel's mother might now have been Bathsheba who orally passed the family heritage of Ruth's spotless reputation along to David's son Solomon. Lemuel could have been a family name for Solomon like Yedidiah who could have penned Proverbs 31:10–31 with Ruth in mind. (*Women of Faith, Bravery and Hope* by J. MacArthur)

In Ruth 3:11 Boaz calls Ruth *eshet hayil*—a "woman of valor." Apart from Proverbs 31, it is the only other time this phrase is used to describe a woman. *Eshet* is the construct form of *isha*, or woman. *Hayil* carries the meaning of power, courage, bravery and heroism. I believe that Ruth is the model for this Proverbs 31 woman, but remember that when Ruth was called a "woman of valor," she was not married, living in poverty with Naomi and working as a gleaner in the fields. Ruth received her strength and honor from the Lord, and He enabled her to live a life of courage and bravery even in those circumstances.

> She girds herself with strength and makes her arms strong.
> —Proverbs 31:17

The Proverbs 31 woman finds her courage and strength from the God of Israel. However, if you are like me you may be intimidated by the list of unrealistic accomplishments this Proverbs 31 woman models. Let's refocus on what this Scripture is truly saying to us as women. Our value does not come from our "to do lists" that run a household or a company. On the contrary, a woman of valor is a measure of spiritual maturity formed in us as we honor the Lord. We are women of courage not by what we do in our own strength but by our dependence upon God each day.

BEHOLD! SOMEONE GREATER THAN SOLOMON IS HERE

The most important section of this closing chapter is about how King Solomon's life prefigures the ministry of Yeshua the Messiah. The Hebrew Scriptures declare that Solomon was the greatest king of his time. Everyone sought his Godly wisdom.

> So King Solomon became greater than all the kings of the earth in riches and in wisdom. And all the earth was seeking the presence of Solomon, to hear his wisdom which God had put in his heart.
> —1 Kings 10:23–24

BATHSHEBA

Even the Queen of Sheba travelled a great distance to hear what Solomon had to say. It is fascinating that Yeshua references the Queen of Sheba's visit hundreds of years later during His earthly ministry, when He addressed the unbelieving crowds who demanded a sign from heaven to prove Yeshua's authenticity.

First Yeshua speaks to them about the sign of Jonah.

> Yeshua answered, "A wicked and adulterous generation asks for a sign! But none will be given it except the sign of the prophet Jonah. For as Jonah was three days and three nights in the belly of a huge fish, so the Son of Man will be three days and three nights in the heart of the earth. The men of Nineveh will stand up at the judgment with this generation and condemn it; for they repented at the preaching of Jonah, and now something greater than Jonah is here."
> —Matthew 12:38–41 (NIV)

Yeshua is comparing His death, burial and resurrection with the three days that Jonah spent inside the great fish. He also says that they will be judged by the standard of the Ninevites who, when they were confronted with their sin, repented and trusted in God. Yeshua follows that with the illustration of the Queen of Sheba as He challenges his accusers.

> The Queen of the South shall rise up with this generation at the judgment and shall condemn it, because she came from the ends of the earth to hear the wisdom of Solomon; and behold, something greater than Solomon is here. —Matthew 12:42

Why would Yeshua bring up the Queen of Sheba? First, she had traveled a great distance just to listen to the wisdom of Solomon. These crowds, spouting off their challenges and accusations did not have to travel from afar to hear Yeshua, but rather had seen His many miracles and heard His teachings in their hometowns. Still they treated him disrespectfully.

What a different response Solomon received from the Queen of Sheba.

> Then she said to the king, "It was a true report which I heard in my own land about your words and your wisdom. "Nevertheless I did not believe the reports, until I came and my eyes had seen

it. And behold, the half was not told me. You exceed in wisdom and prosperity the report which I heard."
—1 Kings 10:6–7

Blessed be the LORD your God who delighted in you to set you on the throne of Israel; because the LORD loved Israel forever, therefore He made you king, to do justice and righteousness.
—1 Kings 10:9

In Yeshua's rebuke of this crowd who had gathered to accuse him, he says that the Queen of Sheba, a Gentile who became a follower of the God of Israel, would rise up and pass judgment on them. Why? Yeshua declares,

"Behold, someone greater than Solomon is here."
—Matthew 12:42b

How is Yeshua Greater than Solomon?

Yeshua is greater than Solomon in every way. Solomon was an earthly king who received his wisdom from a higher authority. In the book of Revelation Yeshua is proclaimed to be the KING OF KINGS and LORD OF LORDS! He is the One returning with us to judge all His enemies and establish righteousness for eternity.

And on His robe and on His thigh He has a name written, "KING OF KINGS and LORD OF LORDS." —Revelation 19:16

Yeshua, as our King blesses us.

Blessed be the God and Father of our Lord Yeshua the Messiah, who has blessed us with every spiritual blessing in the heavenly places in Messiah. —Ephesians 1:3

He lavishes wisdom on all His children.

In Him we have redemption through His blood, the forgiveness of our trespasses, according to the riches of His grace, which He lavished upon us. In all wisdom and insight. —Ephesians 1:7

BATHSHEBA

We have continual, confident access into the presence of our King and High Priest:

> Since then we have a great high priest who has passed through the heavens, Yeshua the Son of God, let us hold fast our confession. For we do not have a high priest who cannot sympathize with our weaknesses, but One who has been tempted in all things as we are, yet without sin. Let us therefore draw near with confidence to the throne of grace, that we may receive mercy and may find grace to help in time of need. — Hebrews 4:14–16

Yeshua is the Living Word and you have the mind of Messiah your King.

> For who has known the mind of the Lord, that he should instruct Him? But we have the mind of Messiah. —1 Corinthians 2:16

Yeshua is in Charge of Peace because He is the Prince of Peace

Solomon's name may mean "Man of Peace," but at the end of his rule his kingdom was anything but peaceful, as it split into two kingdoms shortly after his death. In contrast, Yeshua is the Prince of Peace, a Messianic title found in the writings of Isaiah.

> For a child will be born to us, a son will be given to us; And the government will rest on His shoulders; And His name will be called Wonderful Counselor, Mighty God, Eternal Father, Prince of Peace (*Sar Shalom*). —Isaiah 9:6

As the Prince of Peace, Yeshua is in charge of bringing Peace to not only the world and also to you personally. When Yeshua taught His disciples about having peace He gave them the key to having His *shalom* as seen in the verses from the Gospel of John.

> Peace I leave with you; My peace I give to you; not as the world gives, do I give to you. Let not your heart be troubled, nor let it be fearful.
> —John 14:27

COMPASSION *and* REDEMPTION

> These things I have spoken to you, that in Me you may have peace. In the world you have tribulation but take courage; I have overcome the world. —John 16:33

This is not an exhaustive list, but just a beginning to understand how Yeshua is greater than Solomon in every aspect.

Thoughts and Reflections

1. Consider these questions for your own life: Is Yeshua truly in charge of how you are living? Is He your Sovereign Lord and your King? Are you trusting in Him to give you His shalom each day? Yeshua loves you and desires to be your eternal King of Kings and Lord of Lords.

2. Consider that the only other woman who is called "a woman of valor" or eshet hayil is Ruth. Boaz declares to her in Ruth 3:11 "And now, my daughter, do not fear. I will do for you whatever you ask, for all my people in the city know that you are a woman of excellence." How is Ruth's life of courage, faith and loyalty seen in the description of the Proverbs 31 woman?

3. Take time to go over the Scriptures which confirm who Yeshua is as King of Kings and Lord of Lords. Add more passages that are meaningful to you as you mediate on the fact that He is your eternal King.

Our final section will focus on the birth and childhood of the King of Kings and the fifth woman named in Yeshua's genealogy—his mother, Miriam.

SECTION FIVE

מרים
MIRIAM

"Jacob was the father
of Joseph the husband
of Miriam, by whom
was born Yeshua,
who is called Messiah"
Matthew 1:16

13. A Time of Miracles

Miriam, the mother of Yeshua the Messiah, is the fifth and final woman Matthew mentions in his genealogy.

> And to Jacob was born Joseph the husband of Miriam by whom was born Yeshua, who is called the Messiah." Although most people around the world have come to know her as Mary, Miriam is her actual Hebrew name, the name that she would have been known by and responded to in her lifetime therefore, we will be using Miriam's Hebrew name for our study of her life.
> —Matthew 1:16

Miriam was a Jewish teen living in the first century at a time when there was a growing number of Jewish zealots who had a deep Messianic hope. This hope was fixed on the anticipation that the Messiah would deliver them from the oppressive Roman rule. Some of those who were among these zealots are mentioned in the New Covenant: Zacharias and Elizabeth (Luke 1:5–24), Simeon (Luke 2: 25–35) and Anna the prophetess (Luke 2:36).

As we have delved into the lives of the women in Matthew's genealogy, we have seen God's providential care for each one. In Miriam, we will discover how the Lord worked in her life, pouring His grace and mercy out to her.

Once in a Lifetime

In the first chapter of Luke, we find the angel Gabriel announcing Good News of the coming Messiah to certain people chosen by God. His first stop is in the Holy Place of the Temple, where Zacharias, a common priest, was performing his once-in-a-lifetime opportunity to offer the prayers of his people before the Lord at the Altar of Incense. Zacharias was standing in the Holy Place, an area of the Temple completely closed off from the outer courts. The only source of light in the room emanated from the seven-branched Menorah, which illuminated the Table of the Bread of God's Presence and the Altar of Incense, located just outside the thick curtain entrance to the Holy of Holies.

I found this description from the *Easton's Bible Dictionary* helpful in clarifying just how special the timing of this day would have been for Zacharias:

MIRIAM

Zacharias was a priest of the course of *Abia*, eighth of the twenty-four courses into which the priests had been originally divided by David (1 Chronicles 23:1–19). Only four of these courses or "families" of the priests returned from the Exile (Ezra 2:36–39); but they were then redistributed under the old designations. The priests served at the temple twice each year, and only for a week each time. Zacharias' time had come for this service. During this period his home would be one of the chambers set apart for the priests on the sides of the temple ground. The offering of incense was one of the most solemn parts of the daily worship of the temple, and lots were drawn each day to determine who should have this great honor, an honor which no priest could enjoy more than once during his lifetime.

After serving as a priest all his life, in his later years, Zacharias had been chosen to present the prayers of Israel at the Altar of Incense in the Holy Place for this special week of service. As he was preparing to offer the prayers of the multitudes who waited outside in the temple courtyard, the angel Gabriel suddenly appears at the right side of the Altar of Incense. Zacharias had never seen an angel and was understandably terrified. But Gabriel quickly assures Zacharias there was no need to be afraid and follows this assurance with wonderful news.

> "Do not be afraid, Zacharias, for your petition has been heard, and your wife Elizabeth will bear you a son, and you will give him the name John." —Luke 1:13

GOD ALWAYS HEARS YOUR PRAYERS

The Scriptures tell us in Luke 1:7 that Elizabeth was childless, barren, and at this point in her life, much too old to bear children. This makes the announcement all the more miraculous. Not the dreaded angel of death, Gabriel was a messenger of life and hope!

How long do you imagine Elizabeth and Zacharias had prayed to have a child? Do you think that they had stopped asking after Elizabeth grew too old to conceive? By this time, they had most likely accepted the disgrace of childlessness.

Let's stop and consider this for our own lives. Are there prayers and petitions that you have given up on? I know there are deep desires in my heart; but because of my discouragement, I no longer pray about them.

COMPASSION *and* REDEMPTION

Perhaps like me, you have stopped praying. It might be a request for the salvation of an obstinate family member, the rehabilitation of an addicted friend or some long-forgotten aspiration buried in your soul.

This encounter between Zacharias and Gabriel is a reminder that God hears our prayers. In Luke 1:13 Gabriel says, "your petition has been heard." Praying to God is not like petitioning a statue with no power to effect change. When we pray, God not only hears but desires to answer our deepest cries. Problems arise when God's response is not what we expect. The timing of God's reply can also be an issue. Sometimes there is an immediate yes or no. At other times His answer is "not yet." When the "not yet" comes, we can only pray for patience and await His perfect timing. I also pray for grace to accept whatever His answer might be, remembering that God loves me and always has the best plan for my life.

God's Kindness to Zacharias

The promise of a son is great news for Zacharias! At that very moment, in the Holy Place by the Altar of Incense, he is assured that the God he serves is listening to the deep cries of his heart and that of his wife Elizabeth. The angel goes on to explain that their son will not be an ordinary child, but that his birth would cause many to rejoice. Their baby will be great in God's sight and filled with the Holy Spirit, even while he is growing in Elizabeth's womb. He would fulfill the prophecies of Malachi and be the one to prepare the way of the Messiah.

> And it is he who will go as a forerunner before Him in the spirit and power of Elijah, to turn the hearts of the fathers back to the children, and the disobedient to the attitude of the righteous; so as to make ready a people prepared for the Lord. —Luke 1:17

Even though Zacharias was a righteous and faithful priest, his initial response to Gabriel was skepticism.

> How shall I know this for certain? For I am an old man, and my wife is advanced in years. —Luke 1:18

Gabriel tells him that because he did not believe, Zacharias would be unable to speak until his son was born. Can you hear the frustrated messenger's tone in verse 19?

MIRIAM

And the angel answered and said to him, "I am Gabriel, who stands in the presence of God; and I have been sent to speak to you, and to bring you this good news. And behold, you shall be silent and unable to speak until the day when these things take place, because you did not believe my words, which shall be fulfilled in their proper time." —Luke 1:19–20

This response to Zacharias' incredulity may seem a little harsh. A crowd of people waited outside the Holy Place to receive the customary priestly blessing. When he emerged from the Holy Place, the crowds understood that Zacharias, now mute, must have had a vision. They wondered what happened, but Zacharias could not speak. Luke notes that after Zacharias finished his week of service, he returned home to join his wife Elizabeth.

I believe that his silence, rather than being punitive, was a blessing from God. This time of muteness gave Zacharias a time to reflect, pray, and seek the Lord in quietness. After Elizabeth did give birth, Zacharias was the one to give the baby the name that God had undoubtedly revealed to him. He wrote on a tablet, "His name is John" to the astonishment of his family and friends who were gathered for the circumcision. And it was at this very moment that Zacharias regained his speech. The first words uttered were declarations of praise and prophecy as he was filled with the Holy Spirit. (Luke 1:67–79)

When I consider how God dealt with Zacharias, I'm thankful for His continual patience and lovingkindness in my own life. My heart has always been to serve the Lord ever since I moved to New York City as a raw 21 year old in 1968. God always knows when I need to be silent. Over these many years, He has "silenced" me during times of exhaustion, or at moments when I was prone to give in to bad attitudes. In hindsight, I understand that He did this to protect me from situations I was unable to handle. During those times, whether through the occasion of an illness, an injury, or emotional or spiritual emptiness, God gave me the opportunity to be still and remember that He is God.

Thoughts and Reflctions
1. Think of the prayers that you consider unanswerable. Ask the Lord to give you renewed assurance that He will

answer you in His time and according to His purposes for your life.

2. Look up these Scriptures listed and meditate on some of Yeshua's promises regarding prayer: John 14: 12–14, John 15:7–8, John 16:23–24

14. Her Humble Heart Revealed

The fullest account of Miriam's miraculous pregnancy is found in the Gospel of Luke.

> Now in the sixth month the angel Gabriel was sent from God to a city in Galilee, called Nazareth, to a virgin engaged to a man whose name was Joseph, of the descendants of David; and the virgin's name was Miriam. —Luke 1:26–27

What does it mean when the Scripture says that she was "a virgin engaged to a man?" The word engaged is also translated "espoused" or "betrothed" in the King James and the English Standard versions of the Bible. Both of these translations convey the significance of that term. In my book *Eternally Desired*, I explain the four stages of a Jewish wedding and how each stage parallels our relationship with Yeshua as His Bride. The first stage of a Jewish wedding is the "arrangement," the time of choosing one's spouse. The second stage is the "betrothal," which Luke refers to in 1:27. According to Jewish wedding customs, being betrothed means that you are married, though the physical consummation is to take place at a later time.

At the betrothal, the groom signs the ketubah or marriage contract which serves as a promise of the groom's love to his bride. The betrothal begins with a ceremony conducted under the wedding canopy called a chuppah. The groom and bride share a cup of wine and recite the betrothal blessings. The bond of betrothal or engagement is as good as marriage. It is a covenant that cannot be broken.

How did Joseph respond to the news of his fiancée's pregnancy? After finding out she was with child, Joseph planned to divorce her privately because it seemed obvious from her condition that she had dishonored their betrothal. But before he could do this, an angel appeared to Joseph. A man of simple trust in the Lord, Joseph believed God and remained betrothed to Miriam.

Consider what Miriam did while she was waiting for Joseph to come for her. She may not have understood how everything would work out, but she trusted God and she trusted her groom. How relieved she must have been when the angel interceded on her behalf and let Joseph know that she had become pregnant by God's Spirit. The unexplained mystery and miracle of her pregnancy tried their betrothal bond, yet the angel came at just the right time to strengthen it again. Understanding the significance of their supernatural circumstances, Joseph and Miriam do not consummate their marriage until after Yeshua is born.

Why was Miriam Chosen?

In the Jewish culture of the first century, having children was understood to be a blessing from God. Accordingly, the woman chosen to give birth to the Messiah of Israel would have been given the ultimate honor and the ultimate blessing! But why did He choose Miriam? I believe that like Tamar, Rahab, Ruth and Bathsheba, Miriam needed God's grace. Luke chapter one will help us find answer as Gabriel greets Miriam,

> "Rejoice highly favored one! The Lord is with you."
> —Luke 1:28 (NKJV)

Rejoice in Greek is *chairo* which means "glad." So right from the start Gabriel is announcing joyful news. Favored one comes from a similar Greek word charitoo: "endowed with grace." In other words, "Miriam, be glad, because God sees you through His grace and He is with you." Sounds like a great beginning, doesn't it? However, Miriam's initial response reveals that she was afraid and could not understand how she could be favored by God.

> But she was greatly troubled at this statement, and kept pondering what kind of salutation this might be. —Luke 1:29

But the angel kept reassuring her.

> Do not be afraid, Miriam; for you have found favor with God. And behold, you will conceive in your womb, and bear a son, and you shall name Him Yeshua. "He will be great, and will be called the Son of the Most High; and the Lord God will give Him the throne of His father David; and He will reign over the house of Jacob forever; and His kingdom will have no end."
> —Luke 1:30-33 (NKJV)

Gabriel has plenty of good news for Miriam as he weaves into his announcement the name Yeshua, meaning "God who saves." Gabriel shares prophecies which Yeshua will fulfill. He will be great, He will be called Son of the most High, He will sit on the throne of David and be King of the Jews forever. All this will be accomplished through the baby that she will carry in her womb. Now Miriam gets practical:

> How can this be, since I am a virgin? —Luke 1:34

Whereas Zacharias' question to Gabriel was rooted in unbelief, it was different for Miriam. As we progress through this portion in Luke, we discover that Miriam's question was founded on faith. Miriam accepts the word of God's messenger; yet, she is confounded by the ways of God. How can she possibly give birth to this son when she has never had sexual intercourse?

Even as she wondered about her virginity, Miriam may have had a glimmer of understanding. Centuries before, the prophet Isaiah foretold that a virgin would conceive and bear a son. That His Name would be called Immanuel, "God with us" (Isaiah 7:14). Miriam may have recalled the promise of a Redeemer given in Genesis 3:15, that spoke of the One who would be born of the seed of a woman and who would crush the head of Satan. Miriam must have wondered how this would all work out.

An Amazing Announcement

Gabriel answers her question.

> The Holy Spirit will come upon you, and the power of the Most High will overshadow you; and for that reason the holy offspring shall be called the Son of God. —Luke 1: 35

When you hear the term "overshadow" what do you think of? Two synonyms for overshadow are "outshine" or "dominate." Think of what was happening to Miriam as the presence of God came to dwell in her. When you are in the shadow of His protection, you are in His safest place.

> He who dwells in the shelter of the Most High will abide in the shadow (the protection) of the Almighty. —Psalm 91:1

> Keep me as the apple of the eye; Hide me in the shadow (shade, protection, shelter) of Thy wings. —Psalm 17:8

COMPASSION *and* REDEMPTION

Nothing is impossible with God
Gabriel has even more news!

> And behold, even your relative Elizabeth has also conceived a son in her old age; and she who was called barren is now in her sixth month. —Luke 1:36

When Gabriel tells Miriam about Elizabeth, it's more than just a casual, "did you hear, your cousin is also with child." God's timing and provision for Miriam demonstrates His understanding of Miriam's needs, physically, emotionally and spiritually.

Gabriel's next proclamation is a statement that should blow our socks off.

> For nothing will be impossible with God." —Luke 1:37

In these few statements, Gabriel places the cherry on the top of this sundae of great news, (or if you are like me, it's dark chocolate ganache with extra whipped cream). Gabriel explains to Miriam that her older cousin, who had been barren all her life, is now six months pregnant. What reassurance: "Elizabeth will be going through this time with you!" God knew how much it would mean for these two women to be sharing this season of miracles together. Miriam would need the support and care of an older woman who could empathize and understand the supernatural nature of it all. During her betrothal period, she would have limited contact with Joseph, giving him time to prepare their new home and awaiting the green light from Joseph's father, to fetch Miriam so they might consummate the marriage under their new roof.

God is all powerful. Nothing is too difficult for Him. This is an overarching theme of the Scriptures. Yet this question, "Is anything too difficult for the LORD?" must be answered repeatedly in our day-to-day walk. We need to remember that this Scriptural certainty is not only true for Abraham, Sarah, and Miriam but for us as well. As children of God, we live supernatural lives where miracles can occur on a daily basis. When I read this chapter of Luke, I can hear Gabriel declare in his most authoritative voice this powerful truth of Scripture: nothing is impossible with God! Can you say it with Gabriel for your own life? Nothing is impossible with God!

MIRIAM

I find it fascinating how often in Scripture God's miraculous power is expressed in the context of miracle births. For skeptics who cannot believe that Yeshua took on human flesh through an immaculate conception, consider that without God intervening over dead wombs, there would have been no Jews at all. The nation of Israel is founded upon numerous accounts of miraculous births. Sarah was barren and way past the age of child bearing. Rebekah and Rachel had tried and failed, till God opened their wombs. Today we can praise the Lord that from the aged Sarah came Isaac, the child of promise through whom would come the nation of Israel. Rebekah gave birth to Jacob; and Rachel had Joseph—all important names in the history of the Jewish people and in the lineage of Messiah.

Now, in Miriam's time, dual miracles of her pregnancy as well as the miracle birth of Zacharias and Elizabeth's son John are crucial to the New Covenant narrative. John the Baptizer prepares the way of the Lord in the spirit of Elijah, as the forerunner of Yeshua the Messiah.

God is the One who opens wombs and closes wombs.

> Behold, children are a gift of the LORD; The fruit of the womb is a reward. —Psalm 127:3

THE FATHER OF COMPASSION

There is one name for God that I personally find encouraging, especially when we are thinking about our wombs. The name is *Av HaRachamim*, "The Father of Mercies" or "The Father of Compassion." The word (*av*) means father. The word compassion is from the Hebrew root, *rechem* which is translated womb.

Whenever God is called The Father of Compassion, "compassion," *rachamim*, is always in the plural form. This plural tells us that God doesn't just dole out just a single drop of mercy at a time. Rather, His endless compassions are new every morning. They are always in abundance whenever we seek God's face and His kindnesses. (Lamentations 3:19–26)

It is noteworthy that the root word for rachamim is rechem (womb). This comfort, from *Av HaRachamim*, the Father of Compassion, is likened to the safety and wellbeing of a mother's womb, and points to God's character and care in creating women. God uniquely formed us and gave us the ability to bear children. We are fearfully and wonderfully designed by God with wombs not only to carry new life, but also

COMPASSION *and* REDEMPTION

bring this new life into the world. According to King David, the Lord is intimately acquainted with each of us and the babies that we carry in our wombs.

> For you created my inmost being; you knit me together in my mother's womb. I praise you because I am fearfully and wonderfully made; your works are wonderful, I know that full well. My frame was not hidden from you when I was made in the secret place, when I was woven together in the depths of the earth. Your eyes saw my unformed body; all the days ordained for me were written in your book before one of them came to be. How precious to me are your thoughts, God! How vast is the sum of them!
> — Psalm 139:13–17 (NIV)

WE HAVE HIS MERCIES TO GIVE TO OTHERS

The Apostle Paul knew the Father of Mercies intimately and he wanted to teach those in the congregation in Corinth where to find ultimate comfort in their situations of sorrow:

> Blessed be the God and Father of our Lord Yeshua the Messiah, the Father of mercies and God of all comfort; who comforts us in all our affliction so that we may be able to comfort those who are in any affliction with the comfort with which we ourselves are comforted by God. For just as the sufferings of Messiah are ours in abundance, so also our comfort is abundant through Messiah.
> —2 Corinthians 1:3–5

God knows that we constantly need His comfort as we face the sufferings and difficulties of life. He wants us to go to Him with all our afflictions, not only to find the comfort we need but to share the abundant overflow of His mercy with others.

The same Holy Spirit who overshadowed Miriam's womb dwells in the heart of every believer. Messiah Yeshua encouraged His disciples just before offering Himself on the cross.

> And I will ask the Father, and He will give you another Helper-Comforter, that He may be with you forever; that is the Spirit of truth, whom the world cannot receive, because it does not behold

Him or know Him, but you know Him because He abides with you, and will be in you. I will not leave you as orphans; I will come to you. —John 14:16

The Holy Spirit is called the *parakletos* (comforter, advocate or helper). The Holy Spirit who lives in us offers assurance, comes to our aid and intercedes on our behalf. As Paul taught the Corinthian believers, these mercies are also available to anyone God brings into our lives. We don't have to manufacture fake comfort from our puny resources. We have the power of the Holy Spirit and His endless supply of mercy and comfort.

Miriam's Response

After Gabriel declares that with God all things are possible, Miriam replies,

> Behold, the bondslave (*dolous*) of the Lord; be it done to me according to your word. —Luke 1:38a

Miriam's heart is wide open to the Lord. She sees herself as the Lord's slave and is ready to serve in any way that He desires from her. The Greek word for the phrase "be it done to me" is *genoito*. To get a sense of this word we can look at the Septuagint, a trustworthy Greek translation of the Old Testament. When translating the Hebrew word amen (so be it, in truth, verily) the 70 rabbis who translated the Septuagint often used this affirmative Greek expression "may it be done to me"—*genoito*.

> Blessed be the LORD, the God of Israel, from everlasting to everlasting. Amen, and Amen. (*genoito*) —Psalm 41:13

Amen is a common Hebrew word from the same root as *emunah*, or "faith." When we say amen in response to reading God's words it is a strong affirmation that we believe in what God is saying. Miriam's affirmation, "be it done to me (*genoito*) according to your word" seems to be an expression of faith said without hesitation or reservation. She is ready to submit and serve according to God's instructions.

We must continually ask ourselves if our response to the Lord is *amen* or are we uncertain that we can trust in Him in every difficulty? Ask yourself, "Do I yield my heart to God's words to me with both submission and readiness?"

Her humble heart could be one reason why God chose Miriam. Although she has become one of the most exalted women in the history of the world, it is not because of anything mighty that she accomplished in her own strength, but because she trusted God.

> For thus says the high and exalted One Who lives forever, whose name is Holy, "I dwell on a high and holy place, And also with the contrite and lowly of spirit In order to revive the spirit of the lowly And to revive the heart of the contrite." —Isaiah 57:15

Yeshua of Nazareth, the High and Exalted Messiah, entered the world through the humble womb of a teenage woman.

> And the Word became flesh, and dwelt among us, and we beheld His glory, glory as of the only begotten from the Father, full of grace and truth. —John 1:14

Dancing for Joy

After her encounter with Gabriel, Miriam rushes over to see her cousin Elizabeth, whose exuberant greeting is immortalized in Scripture.

> And it came about that when Elizabeth heard Miriam's greeting, the baby leaped in her womb; and Elizabeth was filled with the Holy Spirit. And she (Elizabeth) cried out with a loud voice, and said, "Blessed among women are you, and blessed is the fruit of your womb! "And how has it happened to me, that the mother of my Lord should come to me? "For behold, when the sound of your greeting reached my ears, the baby leaped in my womb for joy. "And blessed is she who believed that there would be a fulfillment of what had been spoken to her by the Lord."
> —Luke 1:41–45

Not only was her baby filled with the Holy Spirit, but Elizabeth was too, as a celebration of joy erupted in Elizabeth's womb and she was filled with the Holy Spirit. In fact it was a dance party, because in verse 44, the word "leap," synonymous with "dance" or "skip for joy" is used. (Malachi 4:2, Luke 6:23) This response in Elizabeth's womb is a fulfillment of the prophetic words that Gabriel spoke to Zacharias.

MIRIAM

> For he will be great in the sight of the Lord, and he will drink no wine or liquor; and he will be filled with the Holy Spirit, while yet in his mother's womb. —Luke 1:15

Miriam knew that even though Elizabeth was part of this miraculous point in history, the praise that followed from her lips was chiefly for an audience of One, the God of Israel (Luke 1:46–55).

A Magnificent Praise

Miriam begins with praise for the mighty works God already performed, those He is presently doing and what He will accomplish in the future. She engages her own soul and spirit in her adoration of God.

> My soul exalts the Lord, and my spirit has rejoiced in God my Savior. —Luke 1:46, 47

Miriam recognizes that she needs to accept the salvation that only God can provide. This gives her reason to rejoice.

> For He has had regard for the humble state of His bond slave; For behold, from this time on all generations will count me blessed. For the Mighty One has done great things for me; And holy is His name. —Luke 1:48, 49

This blessedness in verse 48 is from the Greek word for happy—*markarious* (*ashrei* in Hebrew). Why would those generations who come after Miriam want to declare her happy or blessed? There was nothing special in Miriam that would warrant such praise. Yet, it was her humility of spirit and her heart of obedience, which the Lord utilized to pour out His undeserved grace into her life. Miriam's happiness is rooted in the fact that God came to dwell in her womb, so she could give birth to the Savior of the world. But after the Messiah was born, she recognizes Him as her Savior and Lord.

> My spirit has rejoiced in God my Savior. —Luke 1:47

Like Miriam, we need to accept the personal salvation that the Messiah offers and enjoy this same happiness that Miriam experienced.

COMPASSION *and* REDEMPTION

HOW TO BE TRULY HAPPY

In the Sermon on the Mount from Matthew 5, (the Beatitudes), Yeshua repeats the same Greek word for happy, makarious, that Miriam used in her psalm of praise. The translation in Matthew 5 can be "Blessed are the..." or "Happy are the..." Four of the Beatitudes in particular point to humility, lowliness, and grief over our sins as the marks of those who are truly happy.

> Happy are the poor in spirit, for theirs is the kingdom of heaven. Happy are those who mourn, for they shall be comforted. Happy are the gentle, for they shall inherit the earth. Happy are those who have been persecuted for the sake of righteousness, for theirs is the kingdom of heaven. —Matthew 5:3–5, 10

This section reminds me of the Limbo dance. Maybe a few of you remember this dance game from birthday parties. The participants are challenged to see how far under the bar they can go without touching it. The refrain of the song is "How low can you go?"

How low can I go? Each morning, if I begin my day in humility, flat on my face before God, I recognize that I must fully depend on His grace to live for Him. This humility of spirit causes me to renew my reliance upon the Lord and then confess my sins. After this I can walk through the day, clothed in His righteousness. I acknowledge that He is in charge, working all things together for my good. I believe this is God's way for me to experience His happiness, the presence of His joy and the fullness of His legacy. After all, in our genealogy of grace we will inherit not only the earth but His Heavenly Kingdom as well.

THE ARM OF THE LORD

As we move through Miriam's song of praise, she echoes the psalms.

> And His mercy is upon generation after generation toward those who fear Him. —Luke 1:50

David wrote these same words of praise for the Lord's mercies.

> But the lovingkindness of the LORD is from everlasting to everlasting on those who fear Him. —Psalm 103:17a

This mercy or lovingkindness (*chesed*) speaks of God's covenant with us. Miriam knew of the covenants He made with her people Israel.

> He has done mighty deeds with His arm; He has scattered those who were proud in the thoughts of their heart. He has brought down rulers from their thrones, And has exalted those who were humble." —Luke 1: 51, 52

The phrase "He has done mighty deeds with His arm" is a direct reference to the Messiah. Miriam's understanding of the coming Messiah and His role is remarkable! The Hebrew word for "arm" is *zeroah*, and in Isaiah 53, we have a prophecy of how the Arm of the Lord would gain the victory through the Messiah's atonement.

Some of us, like my husband Sam, were drawn to consider the claims of Yeshua to be the Messiah of Israel after reading Isaiah 53. Why? Because this portion describes so clearly how Yeshua would grow up in obscurity and be rejected by His own people. Even so, because of His great love for us, He would be led as a silent lamb to die for our sins. The prophet Isaiah begins his chapter with a question.

> Who has believed our message? And to whom has the Arm (*zeroah*) of the LORD been revealed? —Isaiah 53:1

The prophet goes on to describe how He would bear our sins.

> Surely our griefs He Himself bore, and our sorrows He carried; yet we ourselves esteemed Him stricken, Smitten of God, and afflicted. But He was pierced through for our transgressions, He was crushed for our iniquities; the chastening for our well-being fell upon Him, and by His scourging we are healed. All of us like sheep have gone astray, each of us has turned to his own way; but the LORD has caused the iniquity of us all to fall on Him. He was oppressed, and He was afflicted, yet He did not open His mouth; like a lamb that is led to slaughter, and like a sheep that is silent before its shearers, so He did not open His mouth. By oppression and judgment He was taken away; and as for His generation, who considered that He was cut off out of the land of the living, for the transgression of my people to whom the stroke was due? —Isaiah 53:4-8

COMPASSION *and* REDEMPTION

The Messiah of Israel would be rejected by His own people and would suffer and die like a silent sacrificial lamb yet, He would not remain dead. God would raise Him up from the dead. This next portion speaks of Yeshua's burial and resurrection. Do you think Miriam was familiar with this prophecy that the prophet Isaiah penned 700 years earlier?

> His grave was assigned with wicked men, yet He was with a rich man in His death, because He had done no violence, nor was there any deceit in His mouth. But the LORD was pleased to crush Him, putting Him to grief; if He would render Himself as a guilt offering, He will see His offspring, He will prolong His days, and the good pleasure of the LORD will prosper in His hand. As a result of the anguish of His soul, He will see it and be satisfied; by His knowledge the Righteous One, My Servant, will justify the many, as He will bear their iniquities. Therefore, I will allot Him a portion with the great, and He will divide the booty with the strong; because He poured out Himself to death and was numbered with the transgressors; yet He Himself bore the sin of many and interceded for the transgressors. —Isaiah 53:9–12

In Luke 1:51, 52, Miriam proclaims that Messiah would be the one to scatter the proud of heart and bring down the arrogant rulers, thus lifting up the humble of heart as we place our trust in Him.

Psalm 98 also discusses the Arm of the Lord:

> O Sing to the LORD a new song, For He has done wonderful things, His right hand and His holy arm (*zeroah*) have gained the victory for Him. The LORD has made known His salvation; He has revealed His righteousness in the sight of the nations.
> —Psalm 98:1–2

PROCLAIMING GOD'S FAITHFULNESS TO HER PEOPLE

Miriam proclaims that God has given His help to Israel, God's servant. She also praises Him for His mercy to Israel in these final two verses. As a daughter of Abraham, she realizes how important it is that God's mercy and Covenant love be remembered forever. She is declaring that God always keeps His promises.

MIRIAM

> He has given help to Israel His servant, In remembrance of His mercy, As He spoke to our fathers, To Abraham and his offspring forever.
> —Luke 1: 54, 55

Another one of the Psalms might have come to Miriam's mind.

> O seed of Abraham, His servant, O sons of Jacob, His chosen ones! He is the LORD our God; His judgments are in all the earth. He has remembered His covenant forever, the word which He commanded to a thousand generations, The covenant which He made with Abraham, And His oath to Isaac. —Psalm 105:6–9

How Did Miriam Know So Much Scripture?

From the content of Miriam's praise, it is evident that even as a young teen, she was a student of Scripture learning to have a thorough grasp of the Word of God. She includes phrases found in Hannah's prayers from I Samuel 2:1–10. She also echoes truth found in the entire *Tenach*, which includes the law, the prophets and the writings. Luke 1:46–55 contains the most extensive words we have that Miriam spoke during her life, so it's important that we have considered this portion together.

This young Miriam would have heard the Hebrew Scriptures growing up when she went to worship the Lord with her family. I have no doubt that her family and her extended family, including Elizabeth and Zacharias, spent time repeating the promises of God and remembering His goodness every Shabbat. Miriam would have also celebrated God's appointed feasts, which are listed in Leviticus 23.

Nine Months to Trust

When we think of what it was like for Miriam to be pregnant in a small town, we need to consider that she would have been subject to ridicule and misjudgment. Even though Joseph was understanding, it would have been difficult to be out in public. There is no evidence that Miriam ever brooded over the effect that her pregnancy would have on her reputation. It seems that her acceptance of Gabriel's announcement carried her through this time as she submitted to God's will without resistance.

Remember her response in Luke 1:38a? "Behold, the bond slave (*dolous*) of the Lord; be it done to me according to your word." Miriam understood that she was God's servant and that what was happening to

COMPASSION *and* REDEMPTION

her was according to His word. Even her psalm of praise reiterates the promises concerning God from the Hebrew Scriptures. God saw that her humble heart was always seeking after Him. In response, He gave her the understanding, comfort and wisdom she needed to carry the Holy One of Israel in her womb for nine months.

THOUGHTS AND REFLECTIONS

1. How does Miriam's response to the angel Gabriel speak to your heart and life?
2. Meditate on Miriam's psalm of praise in Luke 1:46–55. Then write your own psalm to the Lord as a praise offering to Him. This psalm of Miriam reminds us to always give thanks to God and worship as we take hold of the promises of God.
3. Is there, or has there ever been, a situation in your life where following God brought judgment from others? Can you trust God as Miriam did during such a time? What promises in Scripture can you rely on for encouragement in situations like this?

15. My King of Kings

The location of Messiah's birth was also announced approximately 700 years before it took place.

> But as for you, Bethlehem Ephrathah, too little to be among the clans of Judah, from you One will go forth for Me to be ruler in Israel. His goings forth are from long ago, from the days of eternity. —Micah 5:2

In this tiny town of Bethlehem, the city of David, Miriam gave birth to the Eternal One who would be Ruler in Israel. Much has been written about the humble circumstance of the birth of the King of Israel, and I am always encouraged by those shepherds who were the first to learn of the great news of this birth.

They heard this life-changing announcement while they were tending the sheep at a place called the "tower of the flock" or *Migdal Eder* (Micah 4:8a).

> That the Messiah was to be born in Bethlehem, was a settled conviction. Equally so was the belief that He was to be revealed from Migdal Eder, "the tower of the flock." This Migdal Eder was not the watchtower for the ordinary flocks which pastured on the barren sheep ground beyond Bethlehem, but lay close to the town, on the road to Jerusalem. A passage in the Mishnah leads to the conclusion, that the flocks, which pastured there, were destined for Temple-sacrifices, and, accordingly, that the shepherds, who watched over them, were not ordinary shepherds.[1]

Edersheim, along with many other scholars, offers insight into the Messianic predictions in Micah 5:2 and 4:8. Why did those angels reveal God's glorious announcement to the shepherds first? Not only was this a fulfillment of prophecy but it was also another indication of God using the humble to announce His news of great peace and good will to all men. These were the very people who were keeping those lambs for sacrifice in the Holy Temple. When Messiah was born as the humble King, His destiny was to offer Himself as the Lamb who would take away the sin of the world.

It was a night like any other night as these shepherds at the Migdal Eder were making sure their sheep, destined for Temple sacrifice, were

---
[1] Alfred Edersheim, *The Life and Times of Jesus the Messiah*, 186–87

safe from thieves and predators. I imagine the nights would pass in monotony as they saw to their sheep. However, on this night, something extraordinary would transform their lives forever. The Scriptures note that an angel of the Lord suddenly appeared in the night sky and God's glory lit up the heavens. Can you imagine how bright and how magnificent it must have been? The shepherd's first response was one of great fear; nevertheless, the announcement of good news that followed transformed their fear into wonder.

"Good news" or *euaggelizo* in Greek is often translated as "glad tidings" or "gospel." And what did this gospel contain? First, the news was for everyone because this baby born in David's city would be the Messiah of Israel and the Savior of the world. Furthermore, He is called the deliverer or savior and His credentials rest on the fact that He is the *Mashiach* ("anointed one"), sent by God to fulfill the promises of the Hebrew Scriptures. The miraculous sign that would prove to the shepherds that they had found this Messiah is the fact that He would be a baby in a manger. (Luke 2:8–12)

This good news was initially delivered by the chief angel and then transformed into a party in the skies as a multitude (a lot of angels!) appeared in the heavens praising the Lord. Notice in verse 15 that these shepherds didn't want to miss any of this party, so they waited until the angels were gone to decide what to do. They decided to go to Bethlehem to find this baby and see what this peace on earth and good will to men was all about.

> And suddenly there appeared with the angel a multitude of the heavenly host praising God, and saying, "Glory to God in the highest, And on earth peace among men with whom He is pleased." And it came about when the angels had gone away from them into heaven, that the shepherds began saying to one another, "Let us go straight to Bethlehem then, and see this thing that has happened which the Lord has made known to us." —Luke 2:13–15

Isn't it just like God to use these lowly shepherds to communicate the proclamation to Miriam and Joseph? These shepherd evangelists don't stop there, but they tell that good news to everyone who will listen, spreading the message of the Lord's Anointed One, God's Messiah and our Deliverer. (Luke 2:10–11, 20)

MIRIAM

THE REDEMPTION OF THE FIRST BORN—PIDYAN HABEN

Miriam continued to receive confirmation of all that the Lord was doing through Yeshua her son. She and Joseph took him to the Temple to dedicate Him to the Lord in accordance with the law of Moses.

> Sanctify to Me every first-born, the first offspring of every womb among the sons of Israel, both of man...it belongs to Me.
> —Numbers 18:15

> Every first-born of man among your sons you shall redeem.
> —Exodus 13:2, 13

They consecrate Yeshua with a pair of turtledoves, which was what the Torah prescribed for those who could not afford to bring a lamb. (Luke 2:24) Today this ceremony is traditionally called *Pidyan HaBen*, or Redemption of the Firstborn.

This was to be a very special day because they were to meet Simeon and Anna, two elderly Israelites in the Temple, who had both been longing and praying for the coming of the Messiah of Israel. God revealed to Simeon by the power of the Holy Spirit that the "consolation of Israel" had arrived.

> And behold, there was a man in Jerusalem whose name was Simeon; and this man was righteous and devout, looking for the consolation of Israel; and the Holy Spirit was upon him. And it had been revealed to him by the Holy Spirit that he would not see death before he had seen the Lord's Messiah.   —Luke 2:25–26

Here Simeon reveals the name, "the consolation of Israel" to describe the ministry of Yeshua. This word consolation in Greek is *paraklesis*—the One who comes alongside to help and give comfort. This is the parallel word for the Hebrew, *Rachamim*, from our study of *Av HaRachamim*—the Father of Mercies. When Yeshua came, His comfort and His mercies were abundantly manifested in His ministry. When He ascended to heaven, He gave us the *Ruach HaKodesh*, the Holy Spirit, to be our internal source of comfort.

Then, when Simeon saw Yeshua in the Temple he took Him in his arms and praised God.

COMPASSION *and* REDEMPTION

> "Now Lord, Thou dost let Thy bond-servant depart In peace, according to Thy word; For my eyes have seen Thy salvation, Which Thou hast prepared in the presence of all peoples, A light of revelation to the Gentiles, And the glory of Thy people Israel."
> —Luke 2:29–32

Simeon is ready to die because the Lord has granted his prayer to behold God's salvation, not only for Israel but for the entire world. Simeon is quoting the promise recorded by the prophet Isaiah.

> And now says the LORD, who formed Me from the womb to be His Servant, to bring Jacob back to Him, in order that Israel might be gathered to Him (for I am honored in the sight of the LORD, and My God is My strength), He says, "It is too small a thing that You should be My Servant to raise up the tribes of Jacob, and to restore the preserved ones of Israel; I will also make You a light of the nations So that My salvation may reach to the end of the earth.
> —Isaiah 49:5–6

Both Joseph and Miriam were astonished at what was said about Yeshua. Simeon blesses them but also gives Miriam a prophetic word that she must have kept close to her heart while raising her son.

> And His father and mother were amazed at the things which were being said about Him. And Simeon blessed them, and said to Miriam His mother, "Behold, this Child is appointed for the fall and rise of many in Israel, and for a sign to be opposed and a sword will pierce even your own soul—to the end that thoughts from many hearts may be revealed." —Luke 2:33–35

In hindsight, we understand that years later, as Miriam watched Yeshua suffer and die, her soul would have been pierced through with great anguish. Yet even in her sorrow, she would have remembered the words of Simeon assuring her that all was being fulfilled according to God's plan.

Can we say the same thing as we go through the trials of our lives? If we know the Redeemer and His promises, we can rest on His comfort and His Word to bring us through every situation.

MIRIAM

Anna was a prophetess who served in the Temple night and day and had also received a revelation of the coming Messiah. Then she saw the baby Yeshua.

> At that very moment she came up and began giving thanks to God, and continued to speak of Him to all those who were looking for the redemption of Jerusalem. —Luke 2:38

Where is Yeshua?

Later, in Luke 2 we read that when Yeshua was 12 years old, he accompanied his parents to Jerusalem for the yearly Passover celebration. After the eight-day observance of Passover, the family was returning home. How did the family overlook Yeshua's absence for a whole day? Following the Passover sacrifices, the roads were swollen with crowds returning to their homes. Among them was Yeshua's extended family. The confusion came from assuming that Yeshua was walking with someone else and would eventually turn up. They finally found Yeshua back in the Temple speaking with a group of teachers. All who heard Him were amazed at His understanding. Miriam then speaks to her son.

> And when they (his parents) saw Him, they were astonished; and His mother said to Him, "Son, why have You treated us this way? Behold, your father and I have been anxiously looking for You." And He said to them, "Why is it that you were looking for Me? Did you not know that I had to be in My Father's house?" And they did not understand the statement which He had made to them. And He went down with them and came to Nazareth; and He continued in subjection to them; and His mother treasured all these things in her heart. And Yeshua kept increasing in wisdom and stature, and in favor with God and men. —Luke 2:48–52

Even though Miriam didn't fully understand Yeshua's answer, she did not argue or try to extract an apology. Rather, it says in verse 51 that she "treasured" or kept carefully all that was happening in her heart. Yeshua continued to submit to his parents as He grew in wisdom, maturing and finding grace with God and men. His submitted life must have been a continual reminder to Miriam of His perfect character. His submission is also a testimony to us as we are exhorted to follow in His steps.

COMPASSION *and* REDEMPTION

RAISING THE SINLESS ONE WITH HIS SIBLINGS

Can you imagine what it was like for Miriam to raise a sinless son? It's impossible for me to comprehend what it must have been like for her to be the parent of Yeshua. Miriam had four other sons as well as daughters, as we see from Matthew.

> "Is not this the carpenter's son? Is not His mother called Mary, and His brothers, James and Joseph and Simon and Judas? And His sisters, are they not all with us?" —Matthew 13:55–56

Consequently, Miriam would have dealt with Yeshua's half-brothers and half-sisters as they all grew up together. What a challenge that must have been! Nevertheless, we can be confident that Miriam's strength and bravery for her daily life was rooted in her total trust in the Most High God who had chosen her.

MIRIAM AT YESHUA'S FIRST MIRACLE

During Messiah's first miracle at the wedding in Cana, we have another conversation recorded between Miriam and Yeshua. When the wine ran out earlier than expected, Miriam goes to Yeshua and tells Him that they have no wine. His answer must have come as sort of a surprise.

> "Woman, what does this have to do with me? My hour has not yet come." —John. 2:4 (ESV)

Miriam was not offended but realized that Yeshua was in charge. She instructed the servants "to do whatever He says to do." Miriam was understanding more and more that, like John the Baptizer, she was just the frame that needed to showcase Yeshua as He fulfilled every detail of the picture of God's Redeemer and Messiah.

We don't have any more of Miriam's words recorded in the Gospels. She remained in the background and never sought to intercede for special favors from Yeshua. Several times Yeshua spoke about His relationship with mother and family. As far as His spiritual ministry was concerned, He was clear that His earthly relatives had no more claim on Him that anyone else. This included His mother, Miriam, whom He did not exalt in any way. In Luke 11:27, a woman yells from the crowd to Him, "Blessed is the womb that bore You, and the breasts at which You nursed."

This would have been referring to Miriam. Yeshua answered, "On the contrary, blessed are those who hear the Word of God, and observe it." (Luke 11:28) In other words, Yeshua offers His disciples, including us, a new ancestry. Those who do His will and trust in Him are His true family. No matter our background, we are new creations in Yeshua the Messiah. We are God's sons and daughters.

> But He answered and said to them, "My mother and My brothers are these who hear the Word of God and do it."
> —Matthew 12:47–50; Luke 8:21

In spite of these apparent rejections of His earthly mother and family, Miriam remained one of Yeshua's faithful disciples throughout His ministry and was at the foot of the cross to witness His crucifixion. And Yeshua honored His mother even to His last breath. Just before Yeshua uttered, "It is finished," He saw Miriam standing near John and from the cross said, "Woman, behold, your son." Then He said to John, "Behold, your mother." From then on, John took Miriam into his household to care for her. (John 19:25–27).

From the beginning, Miriam knew that her life as the mother of the Messiah would not be an easy road to travel. Messiah often spoke of the fact that He would die for sins. When Luke wrote his Gospel, it's likely that he went to Miriam for details and eye-witness accounts of Yeshua's birth and His life. She would have spent time recalling those memories which she had treasured in her heart.

In conclusion, Miriam was chosen to carry the Messiah in her womb and give birth to Him. There was nothing in and of herself that was special. She was an ordinary Jewish teen who grew in maturity as a mother and wife, but she still needed a Savior every day. Just as God used Miriam in extraordinary ways, He will use you. As you submit your life to the God of Israel He will pour His grace out to you each day. Remember that the will of God will never take you where the grace of God will not sustain you.

Thoughts and Considerations:
1. Take some time to read and reflect upon Yeshua's birth found in Luke 2. Take time to give thanks to the Lord for sending His Son, the "consolation of Israel" and the comforter for your life through the Holy Spirit of God.

2. In Philippians 2:1–16, Paul describes how Yeshua humbled Himself to take on human flesh. After reading and meditating on this section of Scripture ask God to show you how you can apply these truths in your own life.
3. What does it mean to you that you are eternally accepted by Yeshua and His royal heir of the King of Kings?

Some Concluding Thoughts

We have arrived at the end of this book, and I want to thank you for studying with me as we discovered together how the Lord revealed His grace in the lives of Tamar, Rahab, Ruth, Bathsheba and Miriam.

We also looked at these women's sons and how each of them prefigured the Messiah of Israel—with the exception of Yeshua who is the Messiah Himself. Yeshua is the Bondage Breaker, our Hero and Redeemer, the Perfect Servant, and the Prince of Peace. He fulfills all of biblical history, because history is HIS STORY, revealing Yeshua from cover to cover in both the Hebrew Scriptures and the New Covenant.

As You Are Waiting for His Return

At His first coming, Yeshua entered this time-space continuum as a tiny frail baby, then lived His life ministering as the humble servant however; at His second coming it will be different. He will return as the King of Kings.

> Therefore, also God highly exalted Him, and bestowed on Him the name which is above every Name, that at the Name of Yeshua every knee should bow, of those who are in heaven, and on earth, and under the earth, and that every tongue should confess that Yeshua the Messiah is Lord, to the glory of God the Father.
> —Philippians 2:9–11

What a time we have to look forward to; but, while we are still here on earth, Yeshua reminds us not to be troubled. In fact, the most frequent exhortation that Yeshua gave during His earthly ministry had to do with telling His followers not to be afraid. "Fear not" (John 12:15) and "don't be anxious about anything." (Philippians 4:6) Over and over He says that if we put Him and His kingdom first, everything else will be added to us. Why do you think that Messiah had to remind His disciples so often to "not be afraid, and don't let your hearts be troubled?" (John 14:1) Today, we can be just as fearful and insecure as the believers of the first century.

In fact, we have many of the same concerns as the women in Matthew's genealogy. And like them, we have His assurance of His grace in our lives. Messiah's genealogy proves that Yeshua came to redeem Jews and Gentiles together. Even the so-called "throw away people" are chosen to become children of God.

I pray that your love for Yeshua has deepened during our time together in His Word and that each day you will choose to view yourself accepted fully into His eternal family and born again into His genealogy of grace. He is your eternal King. He is coming back for you very soon.

In closing I am including my ancestry according to the Word of God by personalizing the Scriptures that substantiate my genealogy. Like the five we have studied, I too am chosen to be in His Royal lineage. Take time to personalize your genealogy based on these passages from Ephesians, Romans and 1 John. Ask the Lord to help you grow in your understanding of your own ancestry based on God's promises to you.

My Genealogy of Grace—MyAncestry.WordofGod
#IamHisDaughter
#Miriam'spersonalparaphrase
#It'sAlwaysPersonalwithGod

Blessed be the God and Father of my Lord Yeshua the Messiah, who has blessed me with every spiritual blessing in the heavenly places in Messiah. He chose me in the Messiah before the foundation of the world, to be holy and blameless before Him: in love He predestined me for adoption as His daughter through Messiah Yeshua, in keeping with the good pleasure of His will to the glorious praise of His grace, with which He favored me through my Beloved. —Ephesians 1:3–6

For all who are being led by the Spirit of God, these are children of God. For I have not received a spirit of slavery leading to fear again, but I have received a spirit of adoption as His daughter by which I cry out, "Abba! Father!" The Spirit Himself bears witness with my spirit that I am a child of God.   —Romans 8:14–16

COMPASSION *and* REDEMPTION

See how glorious a love the Father has given to me, that I should be called His child, His daughter—and so I am! The reason the world does not know me is that it did not know Him. Beloved, now I am a child of God; and it has not yet been revealed what I will be, but I know that when He is revealed, I will be like Him, for I will see Him as He is. and everyone who has this hope in Him purifies himself, just as He is pure. —1 John 3:2–3

BIBLIOGRAPHY

Baker's Evangelical Dictionary of Biblical Theology, Edited by Walter A. Elwell, Baker Books, 1996 (in a footnote page 3 in first section)

Bauckham, Richard, *Gospel Women: Studies of the Named Women in the Gospels*. Eerdmans, 2002

Edersheim, Alfred, *The Life and Times of Jesus the Messiah*, MacDonald Publishing Company

Harris, Robert Laird, Archer, Gleason L., Jr., Waltke, Bruce K., *Theological Wordbook of the Old Testament*, Moody. 1980

MacArthur, John, *Twelve Extraordinary Women*, Thomas Nelson, Inc. 2005

Mazar, Eilat, *The Palace of Kind David: Excavations at the Summit of the City of David*, Shoham Academic Research and Publications, 2009

Meyer, F. B., *David: Shepherd, Psalmist, King*, Christian Literature Crusade, 1977

Nadler, Sam, *The Book of Ruth: Hope Fulfilled in the Redeemer's Grace*, Word of Messiah Ministries, 2006

Nadler, Miriam, *Eternally Desired*, Word of Messiah Ministries, 2014

Nadler, Miriam, *Honoring God with My Life*, Word of Messiah Ministries, 2012

Phillips, John, *Exploring Genesis*, Kregel Publications, 2001

The Preacher's Outline and Sermon Bible, Leadership Ministries Worldwide, 1996–2014

Wiersbe, Warren, *Bible Expository Commentary*: BE Series, Victor Books, Cook Communications Ministries, 1991–2005

ALSO BY MIRIAM NADLER

HONORING GOD WITH MY LIFE:
ISSUES OF SENSE AND SENSIBILITY

Do you want to live a life of true satisfaction? In this study of Titus 2:3–5, you will discover how to live a life according to God's calling and His design. Whether you are younger or older, you can fulfill your Divine purpose and calling as a woman, wife, mother, grandmother and friend. You will enjoy meeting women of the Bible like Hannah, Abigail, Lydia, and Tabitha who serve as examples to all of us. This study is meant to help you grow and mature in the godly qualities found in Titus 2:3-5, and also equip you to mentor and disciple other women. (200 pages)

ABIDING IN MESSIAH: BEARING FRUIT IN YESHUA

Learn what matters most to God and discover a life of significance through abiding in Yeshua the Messiah. Beginning with Israel as the vineyard of the Lord in Isaiah 5, study the tender care the Keeper of the vineyard provides His people. Take a deeper look at the words of Yeshua to His disciples in John 15:1: "I am the true vine, and My Father is the Keeper of the vineyard." You will find deeper joy in your relationship with Yeshua as you understand what it means to abide in Him as well as to stand firm in His armor in the midst of spiritual warfare. 118 pages

ETERNALLY DESIRED:
LIVING OUT YOUR VALUE IN YESHUA

The Scriptures are filled with metaphors and symbols God uses to communicate eternal truths. The symbol of the bride of Messiah and the wedding ceremony is woven throughout the fabric of the Hebrew Scriptures and the New Covenant. Here we explore the customs of the ancient Jewish wedding and their parallel with Scripture. Since a wedding is one of the most joyful events in life, it serves as a perfect way to understand the joy, provision, and security of His love towards those who are in Messiah. As His bride, each one of us is eternally desired by Him. Your Groom, Yeshua (Jesus), has chosen you to be His own special treasure. 117 pages

For a complete list of books and resources visit www.WordofMessiah.org

TO SCHEDULE MIRIAM

Word of Messiah Women's Ministries, led by Miriam Nadler, ministers to women of all ages and from various walks of life, presenting God's Word from a Jewish frame of reference for women's retreats, Bible studies, and seminars. The teaching format can be adapted to accommodate the requirements of your event: a single message, a day seminar, or multiple sessions. Her books are designed to be used for group studies as well as one-on-one discipleship sessions.

For more information about scheduling Miriam, please contact info@wordofmessiah.org or call the Word of Messiah offices at 704 544-1948.

About the Cover

The crown is a symbol of royalty. As long as there have been monarchs there has been self-identifying head coverings to single them out. Purple, a color associated with royalty dominates the design. The details of the crowns worn by King David or King Messiah are unknown to us and the artwork on our cover is not literal but representational, a way to express the idea without getting lost in the particulars. The message we are trying to convey is that the women celebrated in this book are members of the royal line of the Messiah of Israel.

The names of these singular women appear in both English and in Hebrew. The abstract crown has been divided into five vertical strips, offering each woman her royal portion. The strips are shifted up or down to remind us that, although they are discussed together, they lived in very different eras. Yet in spite of the diversity of their circumstances and backgrounds, they are all brought together in the opening chapter of the Book of Matthew, where the lineage of Messiah Yeshua unites their stories, their offspring and their legacies for all time. Thank you for celebrating their lives together in this study.

Dr. Whatly
Josh dentist
256-724-3120